Pilgrimage
to
Personhood

Pilgrimage
to
Personhood

by
Fount Shults

Pilgrimage
to
Personhood

I.S.B.N. 0-914903-20-9

Printed in the United States of America

Published by:

Destiny Image Publishers
Post Office Box 351
Shippensburg, PA 17257
For Worldwide Distribution

To My Mother

who is hardly mentioned in this book but whose prayers and dedication sustained me during those difficult years.

TABLE OF CONTENTS

LIST OF DIAGRAMS

PREFACE

This is a book about images, the self-image, the world-image and the God-image, how they develop and how they can change. It is about birth and growth. It is about the development of the individual in his or her search for personhood. It is about relationships and how one is affected by the "important others" in his or her life. It is about behavior, why one does what he or she does and how that can all be changed. It is about the stumbling blocks and pitfalls one faces on the journey of life.

This is a book for those who desire to experience a radical change on the deepest level of their inner being. One thing should be made clear from the very beginning. This is not a do-it-yourself kit for self improvement. As many have discovered, the self which needs improvement is not adequate to the task. "Nothing good dwells within me, that is, in my flesh", wrote the apostle Paul. "I can will what is right but I cannot do it" (Rom. 7:18). Anyone who begins to read this book with any vestige of hope in his or her ability to make basic improvements through self-effort might do better to lay it aside until life has proven otherwise.

This is a book of hope for those who have given up hope in self-improvement techniques. Many methods have been presented to the public with varied degrees of success. It is true that, by engaging in certain activities, one can begin to feel better about oneself and may even begin to produce signs of success as the world measures success. But, with all the glitter and cover-up, the self which one feels better about, and which has produced external changes, remains untouched and unchanged in its basic nature. It is still self-centered, self-directed and self-sufficient. There is a way out of all that.

The question of credentials might arise in the minds of some readers. "Why is a man with a Ph.D. in the Hebrew language writing a book on the self and its images? Does he think that over 20 years of experience teaching the Bible and related subjects on various college campuses qualifies him for this task?'' By what right do I address myself to this topic? I present myself to you as a fellow traveler, as one who has been there—on the mountain and in the valley, in the caves and in the rocks, in the desert and in the sea, in both troubled waters and in the calm. Although I have no formal training in psychology and counselling, people have been coming to me for counsel, for direction and for encouragement in their journey over the past 25 years or more. Some have been helped.

In seeking better ways to find my own direction and to lead others through difficult times I have read from the works of Freud, Jung, Adler, Rogers, Glasser, May, Berne, Harris, Kelsey, Sanford and many other lesser known names. But my reading in this field has not been as a scholar. I was seeking for personal answers for personal conflicts. For all the interesting and valuable insights received from all those authors, each in his own way significant, I am very grateful. But, with all honesty, I must say that the only book which has given me any real and enduring help is one which has stood the test of many shifting winds and turning tides. I refer to the Bible. I have quoted regularly from the *Revised Standard Version* because it is the version with which I am most familiar.

This is my story. It has many biographical elements, but it is not intended to be a biography. It is presented with an imaginative element with a view of lifting it from the level of purely individual experience to a level of expression which will speak to as broad an audience as possible. It is hoped that this will also become your story as you read the details of your own life into the images and even between the lines. So I invite you to reminisce as you join me in the images of my journey.

A statement of gratitude is in order for my wife, Lynda, whose tireless efforts in working through my scribbling finally produced a typed manuscript. I am grateful to the many who, having heard portions of this material presented in various seminars and retreats, encouraged me to put it in written form, and those who have read various portions and offered valuable suggestions. I must take full responsibility for the content. Whether that be an honor or a dishonor will be left to the judgment of the reader.

Pilgrimage
to
Personhood

1

BEING AND BECOMING

Who Am I Really?

I was alone, but not lonely. The electronics school at Keesler Air Force Base had been in session for several weeks and we had our first weekend off. We were all ready for a break. Most of my buddies were seeking diversion through partying. My upbringing would not have allowed me to enjoy the party. Beyond that, however, I wanted to be alone. Some of the basic questions of life were beginning to press their way into the front of my mind. So I went to the beach to think. There was a quiet expectation, a sense that something, or someone, was going to meet me there.

As I waded barefoot in the Gulf of Mexico, just outside Biloxi, Mississippi, the warm gentle waves and the movement of the sand under my feet began to settle whatever anxieties were lingering. There were other people on the beach but it was not crowded. I may just as well have been alone, no one took notice of my presence. As my soul was quieted, my attention was focused completely on the inner event which was gradually ebbing its way into my consciousness.

"It's good to be away from home," I thought. I felt free to

be me—to become whatever I could become—without having to answer to my family. There was no desire to rebel against anything; I just felt a release from pressures which I had known all my life. The pressure of trying to live up to the expectations of others, and feeling so inadequate, had taken its toll on my inner development. I had never been able to please my father no matter how hard I tried (at least that is how I felt). Now I was free from all that (at least that is what I thought).

With this new sense of freedom, however, new questions began to wash over me like waves coming in with the tide. "Free to be what? Free to become what?" I felt a definite sense of awe as the seriousness of these questions began to seep into my consciousness.

"Maybe in me there is something like an acorn." The thought amused me at first. "The whole mighty oak tree is locked up in that little seed. With the right conditions, over a period of time, the full potential of that acorn will become a reality." Hope began to well up within me. "Perhaps there is within me some mysterious kernel waiting for the right conditions to break forth into greatness." This idea hovered over me while something within, beneath the surface of consciousness, was awakened and began to stir.

"It is not as simple for people as it is for trees." As this thought occurred to me some clouds had begun to form and the waves were swelling. "What will come from the acorn is, for the most part, pre-determined; it has no choice. But a man's destiny is affected by the decisions he makes every day."

That "something within" seemed to have suddenly acquired a life of its own, though somehow I knew it had been there a long time. But what (or who) was that? What was the potential of that life which was hidden beneath the surface? There was a sense of excitement as I thought about the possibilities of what I might be able to become. The excitement was countered by anxiety as it occurred to me that it might be possible for a man to waste most of his life trying to become something which he could never be—like a pine cone trying to become an oak tree. I realized that if I did not choose my goals according to my potential I could easily waste my life in frustration trying to become what I could never be.

"Before I decide what I want to become, I must first discover who I am." The Gulf Breeze was becoming a wind. The waves were beginning to attack the shore. The question arose as though from sleep, "Who am I really?"

"The son of Bill and Mildred Shults." I was talking to myself under my breath.

"Right, but who am I?" Yesterday's answers were no longer satisfying. I wanted something more definite.

"One of six children, the second boy."

"Yes, but who am I? Who am I in my own right? What potential is hidden within? What can I become?"

"A former art major from The University of New Mexico, presently in training to become an electronics technician for the United States Air Force."

"True, but who is the 'me' that is living inside and what kind of 'tree' is he destined to become?" My concern was not so much what I might be able to accomplish but what I might become as a person.

There seemed to be no answers beyond my identity with my family, past accomplishments and present involvement with the military. I had reached the age of asking; I was not yet at the age of hearing the answers. All I was aware of at that time was a profound sense of becoming.

I was alone, but I was too overwhelmed to be lonely. At that time I thought I was alone in my questioning; at least it was new to me. But there are always others on the "beach," and many have asked themselves these questions at one time or another. In fact, these may be universal considerations which approach the consciousness of each individual as he or she begins the pilgrimage to personhood. But, not everyone will allow these stirrings to become conscious because there is a sense of being threatened by the possibilities of what might be lurking beneath the surface.

Some try to avoid consciousness by establishing their identity with the castles they build in the sand. Many identify themselves with accomplishments which will not pass the test of the changing tides. Others try to gain identity by following ideas and imaginations which change with each passing generation. Like the mist of the passing cloud these imaginations have no more stability than fantasies in flight. People who follow such things seldom stop to ponder how they came to be on the "beach" or what they will be after the breeze blows the clouds away and the tide returns to challenge their castles. So there are casualties on the journey to selfhood. But the possibility of failure must never keep us from moving forward.

In the journey into wholeness, that is, in becoming the person we were born to be, we must always be asking ourselves four basic questions: (1) Where did I come from?, (2) Where am I going?, (3) What is the "world" all about), and (4) What is my source of strength and direction? The first is the question of **whence.** What sort of seed is it which is struggling for survival and expression in my life? The second is the question of **whither.** Is there an ultimate destiny? A Place of belonging and abiding rather than traveling? Which path do I take from here? The third is the question of **where.** What kind of world is this? What are the opposing forces? How does one make things work right? The fourth is the question of **who.** Am I left to myself in this journey or is there a guide? A partner for the path? A friend who has been there before, who has returned to direct me and bring me to that place? In other words, is there a God? If so, who is He? And how can I come to know Him? How can He be **my** God?

Some of the answers may have been there for me on the beach, but only in a whisper. There were some things I needed to learn, some experiences I needed to go through, before I would have ears to hear those answers. In one sense I was on the right track with my questions. We human beings develop and discover our identity through our experiences in relationship with those with whom we walk from whence to whither. Our self-image is bound up with our parentage, our potential and our source, as we conceive them.

In another sense, however, I was not on the right track at all. This "as we conceive them" changes everything. The direction we choose for our pilgrimage is determined by what we **think** the answers are, even though we never consciously ask. By the time we are adults we have long since adopted some basic concepts, or notions, concerning the fundamental questions of life. These basic notions are sometimes called "images" because they operate from below the level of consciousness in the imagination (not referring to fantasy or daydreaming, but to the faculty through which these unconscious images influence our behavior).

Few of us are inclined to take the time or make the effort to sit down and articulate our answers. Therefore we are usually unaware of the influence these images have on our behavior. We continue to fly off the handle and wonder why. We continue to experience anxiety in certain situations for no apparent reason. Those uncontrollable passions regularly return with power and we fall to the same ploy again and again. This happens because the most highly charged images (i.e., those which are the most difficult to resist) are the ones of which we are least conscious. We experience them only as emotions. We tend to think they happen **to** us and we are not responsible for them.

The pilgrimage mentioned above is a journey into dawning consciousness, but it is not merely an inward journey. To become a whole person with a capacity for life in a meaningful sense of the word, we must become increasingly conscious on two levels: we must become aware of what is "in here" and also what is "out there." In other words, we must not only become conscious of the images which influence our thinking, our feeling and our aspiring, we must also become conscious of the world "out there" as it really is. This is important because many of our struggles and frustrations are a result of trying to force reality into the form of our images. We come into collision with reality when we try to make things work out the way we think they "ought" to. As a result of this collision, our projects miscarry or something desirable is destroyed as we press toward our goals. We seldom stop to consider that perhaps our "ought" needs to change.

If these images are as influential and as significant as is suggested here, it becomes ultimately important for us to discover and adopt the images which are true to reality. But how can we know who we really are and what the world is really like? The path to consciousness is not an easy one to travel because we tend to interpret reality by our unconscious (or even our conscious) images rather than judging our images by reality. The meaningful life is therefore a life of constant adjustments. The life which has ceased to be adjustable has ceased to be meaningful; it has ceased to be life.

Our goal is to help the reader to discover the false images which are influencing his or her life and to offer a way out of the old and into the new. Our discussion will begin at the beginning—at birth—and will follow the development of the images as the individual grows through various phases of increasing consciousness. Most of the illustrations will come from my own experiences, not because of any illusion that these experiences are in any way unique or superior, but simply because I know me best. From time to time attention will be given to the way other personality types may have reacted in similar circumstances. Hopefully most readers will be able to find themselves somewhere, even if it is only between the lines.

2

T-SHIRTS

The Self and Its Images

It all began in a little rock house in Lovington, New Mexico. My father was outside greeting the old country doctor who had come to make his services available on this momentous occasion. It was a lazy fall day in 1936. September 15, to be exact. The greeting drifted into an extended conversation as Dad continued to enjoy the fresh morning air. He apparently forgot what the doctor had come for until the noise from the bedroom window attracted the attention of the neighborhood. I was expressing my disapproval of the fact that they had not been present to witness my arrival.

The doctor rushed into the house, went straight to my mother's bedside and gave me my first medical examination. "Baby boy!" was his official diagnosis. It was easy for him to come to that conclusion quickly since I was naked at the time. That was not intentional on my part, I was born that way. Besides, no one told me I was supposed to cover up when others were around. I did not even know I should be embarrassed. I was not even aware that there were "others." This was the age of simply "being." The age of awareness would come in its own time. The "others" would see to that.

A profound question arises even at this, the first event of my life. If my mother had pinned a pink diaper on me before the doctor arrived, would he have pronounced me a baby girl? And if so, would that have changed my gender? Certainly not! What I was wearing, or not wearing, at that time may have influenced the attitudes of others standing by, but it would not have affected the **basic nature** which was "there" even before birth. A person is what he "is" at birth by virtue of what is "given" before birth, and this principle applies beyond the question of gender. **Seed reproduces after its kind.**

Suppose, however, that my mother had really wanted a girl. When the doctor left she may have clothed me in dresses and frills, fancy shoes and pink lace. That obviously would not have changed me into a girl. But if she continued that practice over a period of time it would have influenced the way the community of "others" responded to me. Eventually it would have had an effect upon the way I thought of myself (my self-image), though my basic nature (the "is" which was present at birth) would have remained unchanged.

The truth is that parents put things on their children besides diapers and jeans. There is such a thing as emotional clothing. In the journey to self-awareness there is an age of receiving and "putting on" whatever emotional garment is presented by the parents. This age is devoid of the capacity for questioning. Children believe and receive whatever the important others in their lives present to them about themselves and about the world. That is just what it means to be an infant and a child. It is a vulnerable stage in many ways. These little ones are at the mercy of those who are responsible for their livelihood and training.

Children "put on" the self-image which is offered to them by their parents in much the same way as teenagers (and some older adults) put on T-shirts to identify themselves with a particular group or ideological stance. These images of the self will not change what is basic to the child's nature, but they will definitely influence the behavior patterns which that nature develops as it strives to come into the maturity of self-expression. The tragedy is that children so completely identify with the "T-shirt" which their parents put on them that they begin to think it represents the real self. And this imagined "real self" often becomes an object of self-hate.

For me it went something like this. One day I looked up at my dad and said to myself, "Wow! That guy is really big. He is the strongest and smartest man in the whole world. He knows everything and he can do anything."

Now, as an adult, I know that there were many men much larger and much smarter than my dad. He was only five feet and seven inches tall. I am certainly not naive enough to believe that he actually knew everything, or that he could really do more than anyone else. But he was the strongest and smartest man in the world of my childhood. The point here is that our personalities develop in the context of the world as we see it (or as it is presented to us), not necessarily in accord with things as they really are. The "reality" of any given situation (whatever that may mean) is of little significance to our growing personalities. The major contributing factor in our development is what we **believe** about the way things are.

My dad was a building contractor. He had visions of developing a company—"Shults and Sons", he wanted to call it—so he was pleased that I was a boy. There was no problem of having to wear dresses and lace. But the boy that I **was** did not match the dream of the boy he **wanted.** He tried to put something on me which did not fit. And when I tried to wear it I soon discovered that I would probably never to able to fill the shirt he had designed for me. The fact that I could not wear what he tried to put on me quickly convinced me that there was something wrong with the "is" I was born with. I would never be able to become what Dad wanted me to be.

Dad was probably as frustrated in trying to get me to perform as I was in trying to please him. It never occurred to me that there might be something wrong with Dad's expectations. He was the guy who knew everything. He would not expect something of me which I was not able to do (no little boy would suspect his father of wrong expectations in a situation like this). I knew it was my own inadequacies which were to blame. Dad's attitude seems to have been that I could become the ideal carpenter's son if he would just continue to apply pressure. If Mom had wanted me to be a girl I would not have been any more frustrated trying to become what she wanted. It just was not in me to be a master carpenter.

My journey into self-awareness was further complicated by the omnipresence of a big brother who had what it takes to be a master carpenter. He was the kind of fellow who liked to take over and do whatever needed to be done. I was the kind who had to understand all the ''hows'' and ''whys'' before I began a project. Once I understood how and why, my motivation had been fully satisfied and I had no interest in doing anything. Consequently, when Dad would give us an assignment to work on together, my brother Joe would pitch in and do it while I was trying to discover how and why. Being much too impatient to stop and explain things, he usually ended up doing most of the work.

Now it was fine with me for him to do everything. That gave me more time to consider the meaning of it all. But when Dad came back to inspect our work, my brother did not hesitate to make it clear who had done all the work.

''Fount does not know how to do anything,'' he would explain. ''He just sat around daydreaming.''

''You should know how to do that.'' Dad was always very sure of the things I should be able to do. ''How many times do I have to tell you? You are just dumb, that's all, just dumb.''

There it was, the first article of clothing for my developing self-image, a ''Dumb-Dumb'' T-shirt. That one seemed to fit much better than the ''Master Carpenter'' shirt, so I put it on.

''You could do as well as your big brother,'' he would say, trying to encourage me. ''If only you would apply yourself! You should know how to do that as well as your brother does.''

He was right as far as I could tell. I looked at my T-shirt and it all made sense. A dumb-dumb **should** know, but **does not.** That is what it means to be dumb. Thus, with bowed head and tear dampened cheeks I entered the age of self-awareness wearing my ''Dumb-Dumb'' T-shirt.

In the next few months several other words and phrases were added to my self-image.

"Lazy"—I sewed it on as soon as possible.

"Never-will-amount-to-anything"—I liked that one. It sounded exciting because it had lots of letters in it. I put it on in many different colors.

In all this business of discovering who I was supposed to be in the world, I never stopped to notice that the T-shirt was an identity which was put on me from the outside. Since I was still small and immature the T-shirt obviously fit well, I really was dumb and inadequate compared to Dad and my big brother. They really did understand things and do things better and faster. So I had no reason to doubt that the words on the T-shirt were an accurate representation of my real self at that time.

I later became aware of other little ones like myself who were also wearing T-shirts. The community of big people had arranged a situation where we could get to know one another. It was a large stone building with the words "Grammar School" over the entrance. I did not understand what that meant but it soon became clear what we were all there for. We were supposed to learn how to play the role which was indicated on our T-shirts. I knew that my place in life was to be the "Dumb-Dumb", so I had to learn how to be dumb in as many situations as possible. I knew I could do it. I could be as dumb as the best of them.

It was amazing to me how well we little ones were able to read one another's T-shirts long before we could read what was written in all those books. It was not a terribly bothersome thing to me when the other kids noticed I was dumb. That was all I had known since the light of self-awareness had first begun to glow. The light was still quite dim, so I did not know one should be ashamed of being dumb. I had not yet reached the age of social awareness.

My first day in class was unforgettable. One guy was there with a T-shirt which said, "Trouble-Maker." He was there to learn how to run over everyone and get his own way. He never seemed to notice that others had feelings. In the very back of the room was a little fellow with "Timid" written on his T-shirt. His project was to learn how to receive abuse without coming into open conflict. It was always exciting when those two got together to see how their roles could interact.

Next to me was a girl with "Charming" written on her shirt. She had already learned how to use her charm to her best interest. She only needed to sharpen her ability to lure and entice without getting herself into a position where she would actually have to pay for what she wanted; then she would be ready for the adult world. Then there was "Cry-Baby" who got what she wanted by crying until the teacher had to give in. There was "Always-Right" who never allowed anyone else to win an argument. There were many others who could be mentioned if that were needed, but you have probably already met most of them anyway.

During the first few weeks of school I became aware that the teacher did not understand what we were there for. She seemed to think we wanted to learn how to read and write and play with numbers. At first this was disturbing to me because it would destroy my image if I learned all those things. Then it occurred to me that this would be a perfect environment to actually find confirmation for my image. Since I was dumb no one would expect me to do well anyway, so I decided to go for it.

My big brother had been sick during his first year of school so he repeated the first grade. I was close enough behind in age to join him his second time through. This worked out to both our advantage. He already understood most of the material so he spent his time doing my homework for me. This was good for him because he was learning how to use his "I-Can-Do-It-Better-Than-You" T-shirt to increase his self-esteem and keep others beholden to him. It was good for me because I was learning how to avoid work by being dumb.

After our third year together, the teacher called my mother in for a conference. "Fount's a smart boy," she said, "but he will never learn to do his own work as long as he is in the same class as his brother."

They agreed that I should be held back. Now I was on my own. I would have to prove that I was dumb without my brother's help. I was confident that I would be able to do that, especially since I could add to my credentials the fact that I had repeated the third grade. For the next few years, my brother continued to do my homework for me. He felt he needed more experience showing others that he could "Do it better" before he could graduate into adult life. This served a double purpose for me. I was able to satisfy the teachers and maintain my integrity as a dumb-dumb at the same time.

Another question arises at this point. Why did I feel obligated to prove that I was dumb? Why was I not able to accept the teacher's evaluation, "Fount's a smart boy," and think of the set-back as an opportunity to prove that I was smart? As it turns out the teacher's assessment was probably right since I was able to complete my education through post graduate work. Why could I not see that then? The answers to these questions will become clear as we continue our discussion.

In the context of birth we noticed that the **basic nature** of a child is "given" before birth, and we identified the agent of that nature as **seed.** In using the term "seed" we imply more than what is physically supplied by the sire. We refer to all that comes to an individual through the process of generation whether through mother or father, all the way from primal man (Adam) until now. By the term "basic nature" we speak of human nature as it finds specific expression within a particular individual. This is the reality of what one "is" by nature, whether he or she is consciously aware of it or not (see Fig. #1).

Here, in the context of developing self-awareness, we see that the agent which forms the **self-image** *is the* **word received**, like a T-shirt, from the important others. By this term "word" we imply more than the mere verbiage which is spoken in the child's hearing. Here the term refers to all levels and forms of communication by which the self-image is received by the child. There are both verbal and non-verbal communications which come to the child from the community of others. A good example of verbal communication is when my dad told me I was dumb. The non-verbal is illustrated by the way my brother always did things before I could figure out how or why.

Each of us begins life with a basic nature which is the founda-

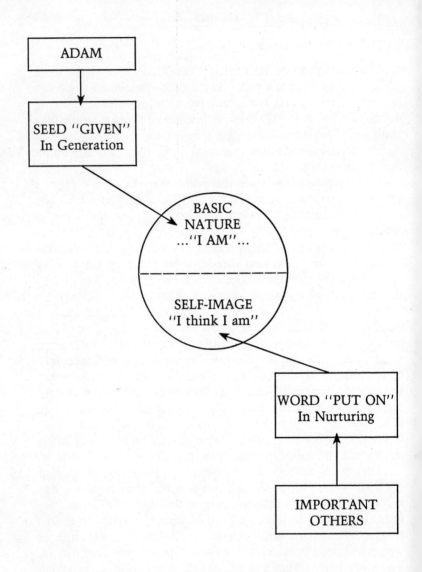

FIGURE #1

THE SEED AND THE WORD

tion from which all development springs. The **first** stage of development we call the **age of receiving.** It is during this time that our basic **self-image** (as distinct from basic nature) is taking form. This formation develops within the context of the interaction between our basic nature and the important others in our lives (e.g., parents and siblings). As the word is given and received the self-image takes form and becomes firmly established. As long as we continue to receive the same communication from the important others, the self-image will remain unchanged.

It is important to emphasize the significance of the word "receive" in this context. We are not suggesting that the self-image can never be changed as long as the same attitudes and expressions are coming from others. The formative element is the word as the child **receives** it, not necessarily the way it is being offered. What he or she receives might be quite different from what is intended by the parents. In the parents' attempt to encourage and give affirmation, the child is often discouraged. On the other hand, there should come a time when one develops to a level of maturity where he or she is able to disregard any inappropriate word of communication from the parents even if it were intended to produce shame and condemnation. When the old word is no longer **received,** one is free to experience change.

We must also give attention to the place of one's basic nature in the development of the self-image. My particular nature, being more docile than resistant, led me to submit to the image of "Dumb-Dumb" and to find ways to demonstrate how dumb I was. Someone more aggressive might have resisted that image and set out to prove it to be false. Even in this case the image of "Dumb-Dumb" has, in fact, been received as a formative element in the development of his self-image. As long as he is trying to prove he is **not** dumb by doing things he would not otherwise do, it is evident that he has received the word "dumb" as a threat, and that he feels obligated to disprove it. When he comes to the point of being able to disregard any implication that he is dumb, when he can go on about his business, then he is free to develop according to what he is in and of himself. He no longer has to prove anything. One becomes a "man" when he is mature enough that he no longer needs to prove he is a man.

The **second** stage of development we call the **age of confirmation.** During this period we tend to interpret situations and statements in terms of the word which we have already accepted (or rejected). For me the prior word was "Dumb-Dumb." I knew I was dumb and interpreted everything that happened as proving that fact. Any event or situation which could not be pressed into the framework of the prior word was simply ignored. An aggressive person under similar circumstances may also have interpreted the various actions and statements from others as implying that he was dumb even though that was not their intent. He would either fight or study harder to prove otherwise; but the word "dumb" would still be a significant factor in his behavior.

During this period we also learn how to manipulate people and situations in such a way as to have external proof of (or opportunity to disprove) the validity of the prior word. We intentionally do things (though usually we are not conscious of our intentions) to elicit a response which we can use to confirm or deny the image we have received. An example of this is the way I would let my brother know that I did not understand something so that he would do my homework for me. What better way could there be to avoid learning and prove my stupidity? For that matter, what better way could my brother have found to prove that he did know? As long as he continued to do all the work I would never learn how and he would become more and more experienced.

For the most part all this is done unconsciously, as we have noticed, but it is this unconscious aspect which gives the images their power. If I had been consciously aware of what I was doing I might have tried to resist the image of dumb-dumb. But, since the image was unconscious, I did not know it was false and, therefore, neither did I know that I might be able to resist its power. It was not until I became aware of the image that I began to have mastery over it. There were several stages of development to pass through before I came to that point.

The **third** stage of development is the **age of longing.** During this time we begin to try to find our place within the social structure beyond the family. This is a time of searching for identity within the group, a time of peer pressures and striving to find some way to be special to someone "out there" among those with whom we are thrown together by the social system, a time of wondering what adult life will really be like, and a time of vascilating between doubt and confidence concerning our ability to be successful in the world into which our growth is thrusting us. This will be the topic of our next chapter.

3

CLOWN SUITS AND CLOSETS

The Longing for Belonging

Was I ever surprised the first time I entered the new school building. I had been excited all summer. The students who had already been through that building said that we would all begin to look like adults and would be trained to behave accordingly. Over those doors were the words "Junior High" and I could hardly wait. Just think, Li'l Dumb-Dumb becoming an adult! The first day of school finally arrived and I came with my dumb-dumb T-shirt all washed and clean.

The surprise came when I looked around at my old friends. Most of them were not wearing their T-shirts anymore. Ol' "Trouble-Maker" was wearing a football jersey with "hero" written on the front. "Timid" was wearing dark glasses and a nice jacket with the word "Cool" across the back. Miss "Charming" was wearing high heels and a satin dress with "High Class" written all over it. It was obvious things would be different this year. The light of social awareness was beginning to shine more brightly.

Then I looked at those who had not yet covered their T-shirts.

In the brighter light, the luster of those old familiar slogans had completely faded. The others had apparently been warned ahead of time that things would be different. They had covered their T-shirts with something more acceptable. I looked at my own and, for the first time, I felt ashamed of being dumb. It would have eased the pain if I had remembered what it was like back behind the veil of clouded memories when I was just "me." By this time I was not even aware of the possibility that the dumb-dumb was not the real me. I had not yet arrived at the age of asking.

Things were changing so rapidly I did not know what to do. It was obvious that I could not allow my T-shirt to be seen in public anymore. After the first few days none of the others were showing theirs either. It was too threatening in the new light. Everyone made fun of you when your T-shirt was showing. It never occurred to any of us that the slogans on our T-shirts could be removed. No, I would have to cover mine like everyone else. Thus, I entered the age of social awareness longing to belong and looking for an appropriate cover-up for my poor self-image.

"What can a dumb-dumb do to cover himself?" The question haunted me until I remembered something. In all my experiences of learning how to do dumb things, people had often laughed at me. In fact, I had come to enjoy making people laugh by doing dumb things. I came to school the next day dressed in my "Clown" suit.

· I soon discovered that one of the main objectives of this phase of training was to select and assume a false identity. We would have to learn how to cover our true feelings before we could receive a certificate of adulthood. Permitting others to know how we actually felt inside was strictly forbidden. It was a cardinal sin to allow an adult to see our feelings (at least in public). At first it confused me that teachers, preachers and parents were allowed to express their feelings. Then I understood that they already had a certificate which said they were adults. They did not have to prove it anymore, at least not to the little people.

Within the various peer groups we continued to help one another with our goals. We took turns doing and saying ugly things to one another to see if we could cause the other to drop his cover and expose his T-shirt. These were good exercises. We were gaining experience in maintaining our false identity in the face of tremendous pressures. The T-shirts were being buried so deeply beneath the surface that it would be a long time before we would have enough courage to ask ourselves the basic question: "Who am I really?" Some never would. By the time the question would begin to press for its own answer the T-shirt image would be so deep as to present itself as the obvious true identity.

My particular disguise offered me a decided advantage during this period of development. I could conceal my embarrassment behind the funny antics and spontaneous skits. With everyone laughing, attention would be drawn away from the fact that I was really dumb. My "ace-in-the-hole" was that, if ever I actually did something dumb (which was quite often; I had learned well), I could cover up by pretending I did that on purpose to make people laugh. This was an adequate answer for those who would accuse me of exposing my T-shirt.

This disguise also afforded me a second advantage. It gave me the illusion of being accepted in the group. Everyone enjoys laughing; so I was always welcome in the various gatherings. I was especially welcome in situations where the big people were putting pressure on us. I could always come up with some funny remark or go through some "Dumb-Dumb" routine and break up the tension. This often got me into trouble with the adults, but it was worth it to have the positive attention of my peers. Deep down inside I suspected they really did not like me, but at least I had all the tokens of acceptance.

As we proceeded through that phase, other changes also evolved. Once we became convinced that we must always keep our undershirts covered, no matter what the cost, the light of the awareness of others slowly grew dim as each began to concentrate upon himself and his own needs. The memory of what the others had been before they donned their disguises also faded. Each of us began to think that he or she was the only one pretending. Everyone else seemed to be so satisfied with themselves and their abilities. And, of course, no one suspected that I was not satisfied with me. We had learned well how to cover it all up.

Now we were ready for the final stage. They moved us to the high school building. At the other end of this phase there were two huge "Brass Doors" through which we would be allowed to pass if we proved ourselves worthy. We were told that on the other side of those doors was the real world of adult life. There was one big room in this school building which was full of books and study desks. They said we would never make it in the real world if we did not learn what was in all those books.

When they described the real world it sounded more like a very big and efficient business office where the only important thing was making a profit. From the way they talked, it was difficult to tell whether the medium of exchange was knowledge or money. I finally figured that money was the ultimate token of acceptability and knowledge was the means to that end. Then I realized something. I would not have to be a master carpenter if I could learn what was in those books.

As I stood in that room with all the books, those huge stacks loomed before me like the well-guarded castle of a sinister old giant. Chills went through my innermost parts. Everything I needed to know to be successful was locked securely behind the covers of those books, and everyone knows that a dumb-dumb does not have a key to unlock all those mysteries. I suddenly realized that my clown suit would be useless in trying to discover all the secrets hidden there on those shelves. How could a dumb-dumb be expected to succeed at a task as foreboding as that? How would I ever be able to make it in the world out there beyond the Brass Doors?

A new kind of longing entered at this point. The prospect of entering a world for which I was so ill-equipped caused me to spend much time in despondency wishing the world were different. I was longing for some utopian world in which people like me could have a place of significance. The truth is that the world is different from my image of it and there can be a "place" for all of us. Only a small portion of the real world is represented by that "business office" image. The teachers obviously talked about many other aspects of life as it would be after graduation, but this particular image was "received" deep within my innermost being and became a threat to me because of my own insecurities and poor self-image. Much of this anxiety and longing could have been avoided if I had understood that I was reacting to an **image** of the world rather than to the **real** world.

This stage is obviously difficult for all concerned. During this age of longing I was so busy trying to gather tokens of acceptance that I seldom stopped long enough to notice that I was really lonely. One reason why I did not notice my loneliness is because I was satisfied with the **illusion** of acceptance. The loneliness itself came from relating to others superficially through the false identity. As a "Clown" I had friends who related to me on that basis, but the "Clown" was not the real me. There was a secret fear which had been almost completely suppressed, but which kept me from opening up to others for any real relationship. It was the fear of being cut off from the group.

A much deeper longing arises when the question comes from deep within: Does anyone like me just for me? Would anyone accept me if I had no tokens? It is difficult to put an age bracket on the rising of this question. Many get trapped within a certain stage and are unable to move on. Sometimes people get caught in a holding pattern for years before they are able to break out. Some never gain enough courage to allow the question to become conscious. The prospect of a negative answer is too threatening. It is a fearful thing to be "cut off from all the living." So we continue to make available what we possess or what we can do in exchange for the illusion of acceptance—until we run out of tokens.

The change of pace in High School helped to ease the pain. With the Brass Doors clearly in view we began to turn our attention to the future. Peer relationships were still important, but the tokens were now being awarded according to what one planned to be when he graduated. Even here there were problems, however, because each one saw the others in the group as having more potential than himself. At best each saw his own potential as less than the image he wanted to present to others.

I looked at those shelves full of books again and thought of my dumb-dumb T-shirt. I knew I would never be able to become anything important, so I set my goal just to get through the Brass Doors. If I could do that, it would be quite an accomplishment for a dumb-dumb. There were many times when I doubted I would make it. But I knew I must get through or I would be exposed as dumb. The pressures continued to mount.

There was also the struggle of trying to keep up the image of "Funny-Man" when other pressures were so great. As I was thinking of taking off the clown suit to concentrate on study, the big question came to the surface. All my friends enjoyed my humor and seemed to like me as long as I was being funny.

"That is nice," I thought, "but I wonder if they would like me if they knew how dumb I really am?"

It seemed that the most important thing in my life at that time was for the "real me" to be loved and accepted for what he "is" rather than for what he could do. I still suspected, in the privacy of my thinking, that the others did not really like me. They only liked the good feeling they had within themselves while they were laughing at the funny things I did. But I had learned to depend upon my sense of humor to collect acceptance tokens. Even though I had an inkling that those tokens were counterfeit, I continued to collect them. The only alternative seemed to be no tokens at all, and that was a fate worse than death.

School became more difficult every day. The things we were expected to understand and remember became more complex and less interesting. Each day the prospect of my T-shirt being exposed was increasing. Retreat seemed the only sensible course of action (a more aggressive person might have intensified his efforts in sports or academics). I found a "closet" in the room with all those books. It was a very special kind of closet where, to anyone looking on from "outside" my little world, I appeared to be studying. On the "inside" I could be enjoying a very exciting adventure.

When I needed company, I would draw pictures of very handsome young men with big muscles and pretty girls who obviously needed a strong man's attention. I would identify myself with the muscle-man and fall madly in love with the pretty girl. She would always get herself into a place of great danger and I would come and save her. This usually required great speed, tremendous feats of strength and sometimes even the ability to fly. But I would always win the girl's eternal affection. I drew the pictures well. It felt good to be needed, even if it was only in my imagination.

One time I decided to come out of my closet and try my hand with a real girl. I chose the one who sat in front of me. I whispered her name and asked, "Do you love me?"

"No." She answered very simply.

"Do you like me?" I was only looking for some kind of positive response from someone outside my closet.

"No." Her answer did not indicate even the slightest interest in the direction of my questions. At that point I really needed some kind of response to reassure me that I had some reason for being around.

"Do you hate me?" I waited for an answer. I would have been satisfied with a "yes" answer. That would at least indicate that I was the object of real attention from someone out there.

"Quite frankly," she responded very calmly, "I never give you a thought one way or the other." I quickly scampered back into my closet. It would be a long time before I would venture out again.

I seldom used the clown suit any more except for occasional social encounters. Since I spent most of my time on those adventures in my closet, the disguise was no longer important. When the last class was over I would move quietly toward the exit giving only those phrases and gestures necessary for the minimum level of acceptability.

The formative element during this age of longing for belonging is a power which we call the **fear of separation.** This fear is related in many ways to the fear of death. There is, however, both a positive and a negative attitude toward death depending on the condition and destiny of the one who is dying. On the positive side there is the notion of the "righteous" who is merely changing his place of belonging from the "living" community to the "sleeping" community. In the Old Testament the phrase, "sleep with the fathers," was often used to indicate this notion. Death could be a comforting thought for those who were confident of being received into another loving community as they were leaving the old one. And it is also true that separation from a group even in this life can be an exciting thing if one knows that the change will bring him into another more promising group.

This confidence is also reflected in Isaiah 57:1,2,

The righteous man perishes
And no one lays it to heart;
Devout men are taken away,
while no one understands.
For the righteous man is taken away from calamity,
He enters into peace;
They rest in their beds
who walk in their uprightness.

Among the Hebrew people, there was **no fear of death** for those righteous men who were confident that there would be **no separation** in death. The issue for them was not death as such, but separation. And the issue of rejection is not rejection as such but the fear of ending up with no "place" in the community.

This positive notion was also reflected in the burial practices of Israel. Joseph insisted that his bones be taken from Egypt to the land of Canaan after his death so that he could be with his "fathers" in the grave. Another example is the statement that Hezekiah was buried in the "chiefest tombs of the sons of David." This was the chronicler's way of recognizing his righteousness. The point here is that he was not separated in death.

The negative side of this notion is often expressed by the phrase, "cut off from the living." This aspect can also be illustrated by the burial practices. Manasseh, the most wicked king in the history of Judah, was not allowed the "comfort" of sleeping with his fathers. He was buried in his own house—**alone.** For him there was a separation from the community at death. The reason attention is drawn to Jezebel's not having a burial may have been to indicate that she was completely cut off at her death. She was not even allowed a "resting place" among the wicked.

This brings us to the first point in our discussion of the fear of separation. It appears that the negative connotations of death come from the prospect of **separation** rather than the fear of death as such. The Israelites feared separation during life as much as they did in death. This is illustrated specifically in the confident affirmation of the context of Psalms 49:15, "God will ransom my soul from the power of Sheol, for He will receive me." The poet was not implying that God would ransom his soul from the inevitability of death. He knew that everyone would at some time face the reality of death. The psalmist expected to be ransomed from the **power** of death, and that power is related to the fear of separation as we will demonstrate shortly.

The significance of this distinction (between death and the fear of separation) will become clear as we consider a definition of death offered by Ruth Paxton in her book, *Life on the Highest Plane*. She quoted Mrs. McDonough, "Death is the falling out of correspondence with environment." Here we begin to see death as a **separation from that environment in which life has its relationships, vitality and meaning.** To illustrate: a leaf has its life and significance within the environment by virtue of its relationship to the tree and the atmosphere. It finds its "meaning" in the operation of receiving light from the sun, carbon dioxide from the air, and in giving oxygen into the air. When fall comes the leaf does not cease to exist, but it no longer corresponds with its environment. It is dead, i.e., separated from its relationships.

The essential element in death, then, is separation. When we look at the larger context of the confident affirmation of Psalms 49:15, we do not see a battle in which the physical well-being of the psalmist was threatened. What we do see is the threat of "men who trust in their wealth, and boast in the abundance of their riches" (v. 6). There seems to have been some threat of separation or rejection based on the measure of the psalmist's possessions as compared to those who were wealthy.

The New Testament also suggests that there is a certain kind of bondage related to the power and the fear of death. "Since therefore the children share in flesh and blood, he himself likewise partook of the same nature, that through death he might destroy him who has the power of death, that is, the devil, and deliver all those who through fear of death were subject to lifelong bondage" (Heb. 2:14,15). Death has power over a man while he is still living. That power operates, at least in part, through fear.

Deliverance from the fear of death comes with the assurance that there will be no separation in death. The one who is confident of being "received" into another (perhaps more significant) community will have no fear of being separated from the one he is now associated with.

We noticed that the broader context of Psalms 49 reveals circumstances which brought the psalmist some cause for fear. Within that situation we also find a hint of how a person might come under the "power of Sheol" in the first place. After a call for the reader to listen, he said, "Why should I fear in times of trouble, when the iniquity of my persecutors surrounds me, men who trust in their wealth and boast of the abundance of their riches?" (Ps. 49:5,6).

The question is put in such a way as to indicate that he was experiencing fear. He was at least acknowledging that one would normally fear in such situations. But why the word fear? It is easy to understand how one would have negative emotions while being surrounded by people who arrogantly flaunt their wealth. One would not quickly identify those negative feelings as fear, however, unless there were more to it than mere boasting. It is apparently understood that the wealthy were using their wealth as a means of separation by rejection.

This brings us to the second point of this study. The power of Sheol can be related to the fear of rejection from the group. The particular form of wealth which the persecutors possessed may not have been so important to the psalmist. What troubled him was that he was being rejected from the "in" crowd because of something he did not have. This would explain how his assurance, "...he will receive me," was a source of encouragement in his encounter with the **power** of Sheol (not

Sheol itself). His negative feelings can thus be identified as fear or, more specifically, the fear of rejection.

When we expand our view of "wealth" to include anything which one might consider to have value, or anything which might become a source of exclusiveness, then we can begin to understand how the power of Sheol operates. My big brother, for example, had a form of wealth which I valued highly as we were growing up. He had our father's attention and approval. He often used his favored position as a means of exalting himself at my expense. This effected my emotional development, because I began to be pulled down into the "pit" of condemnation and feelings of inferiority. This was further complicated by the fact that my father also rejected me much of the time, at least I felt that he did.

The subtle devices of the one who "has the power of death... through fear of death" (Heb. 2:14,15) are exposed here. As we received the negative communication from the important others of our youth, we began to see ourselves as inferior in one way or another. This became a problem when peer relationships began to be an important element in the formation of our behavior patterns. It was at that point that the "power of Sheol" began to exert its secret influence.

Here is how it works. First each one sees the others (which ever group one desires to join) as having something of value which he or she does not have. The apparent advantage of the others then becomes the goal and the absence of that advantage is the ultimate threat. It is an unwritten law that **the supreme penalty is to be cut off from among the "in" crowd.** To be separated from the "living" is a fate worse than physical death. Finally for fear of experiencing this separation the young person begins to do things he or she would not otherwise do.

The result of this behavior (for which the person may secretly condemn himself) is that he begins to close himself off from the voice of his conscience. He would actually rather bare the pressures of guilt than to face the prospect of being openly cut off from his people. He may develop superficial relationships in which he exchanges counterfeit tokens of acceptance for the illusion of being acceptable. The thought that he is not really acceptable (which he may secretly hold to be true) is suppressed beneath the cover of "acceptable" behavior. In so doing—here is the subtlety of Sheol's power—he has chosen to respond to the fear of man rather than the fear of God. Separation from man seems to have more serious consequences than separation from God when one is under the influence of the power of Sheol.

One who follows this course to its end will find that the superficial relationships which he values are built in the sand and will ultimately be faced with the turning of the tide. If he ever tries to do something "different" from the crowd, he will discover that the tokens are in fact counterfeit and that he was never really accepted on any significant level. Having compromised his conscience, betrayed his personal integrity and surrendered his honor, he will also find that he is alienated from himself. Like Jezebel, he may not even be afforded the minimum ceremony of separation. This is a fate worse than death.

The prospect of facing life alienated from the group sets up a dynamic within one's emotional patterns which begins to drive him to seek approval. If a person cannot find that approval within the community into which his family tries to place him, he will be tormented within himself until he finds a place where he can be accepted and approved. It is to this dynamic that we turn our attention next.

4

THE BIG TREEHOUSE

Seeking Security and Success

The final year of training finally came to an end. I was ready to go through the Brass Doors into the real world. I was unsure of what to expect out there, but I was nevertheless eager to leave the room with all those books. Although I was certain I would become a complete failure, I wanted out. I had to graduate.

Appropriate suits had been ordered for all of us to wear at the graduation ceremony. We were all given long black robes so that none of our T-shirts would show. On the front of the robes were these words in capital letters: "I HAVE ARRIVED." They also gave us specially made caps to wear. Attached to the top of the cap was a string which we were to pull as we crossed the stage to go through the Brass Doors. When the string was pulled a flashing light appeared with a little flag which said: "SUCCESS." I knew I had not succeeded at anything, but I was not willing to be exposed at that time. I walked across the stage, pulled the string and went through the Brass Doors.

After graduating from high school, I discovered that things on the other side of the Brass Doors were much different from what we had been told. It was a jungle, not a business office, and the law was the survival of the fittest. It was not efficiency but hardness which brought in the profits. Money was held as the ultimate symbol of success, the most precious token of acceptability. The question of how much a person is worth was answered in terms of assets and liabilities. His abilities were judged by how many tokens came in at the box office. Since money was such a symbol, those who had more used it to enslave those who wanted more.

The means to the end was not knowledge but a combination of cleverness, aggression and a thing called grit. I was sure I had none of those. The only things I had were a clown suit, a photograph of myself wearing the robe of success and that certificate they handed me that said I was an adult. The photograph was already beginning to fade in the heat of the jungle, and I did not know where I had misplaced my certificate. How would I ever be able to prove that I was a jungle-faring man without my certificate? I began to look for a ready-made treehouse which had a clown's position open.

There was no demand for clowns in the jungle unless one wanted to travel with the circus. That prospect had only a slight attraction for me. The idea of making people laugh while the men with the big cigars and canes took all their money did not appeal to me at all. I enjoyed my clown suit in spontaneous situations, but the thought of wearing it permanently was not attractive in any sense of the word, especially since the question of real relationships and true acceptability had come to my attention. But what could a dumb-dumb with a clown suit and a fading photograph do to make a place for himself in the jungle?

As I looked around, it seemed that all the others had enough money to buy all those nice things which make life comfortable and exciting. There I was with nothing, no tokens and no way of collecting any. I learned later that most of the others were actually in debt for all their symbols of success. No one ever told anyone else how many tokens he really had. They just bought as many shiny things as the token masters would allow. That way they could appear to be possessors of many tokens. They seldom took their eyes off the shiny things long enough to notice that they had become slaves of the token masters.

The pretense and cover-up of the early teen years continued in the adult world. Those who learned to play the game well were able to gather many symbols of success and acceptability. Some tried to play honestly, some cheated regularly. But for those who were forced into the jungle system, winning was everything. Somehow the power of the token masters had bewitched them into thinking that winning was more important than integrity or friendship. Of course everyone tried to present themselves outwardly as honest and friendly. The rule was that one is not really dishonest or unfriendly unless he gets caught with his T-shirt exposed.

Discovering the real world beyond the Brass Doors to be a vicious place was a very disheartening experience. I was about to despair when my sister and brother-in-law offered to provide money, with no interest, for me to go to college. I appreciated the offer and was very much encouraged, but I was threatened by the prospect of being a college student.

"A dumb-dumb is certain to be exposed in a university," I pondered, "but here in the jungle I will not only be exposed, I will be eaten alive."

In deciding to accept their offer I certainly did not tell them how threatened I was. As I began to look more closely at the university, however, I found a place where it might be possible for me to hide. In my imaginary closet during high school, I had learned to draw well enough to think that I might be able to make it through college as an art major.

"Art majors are not expected to have a key to unlock all those secrets in the books," I reassured myself. "Besides, with my brother-in-law paying the expenses, I will not have to face the issue of collecting green certificates of success for quite some time yet."

As soon as I arrived on campus I bought a pair of dark glasses, let my hair grow a bit and tried to produce a beard with the five whiskers which appeared on my chin. I wore an old pair of jeans and a worn out sweat-shirt with the word "Beat" on the front and back. The "beat" generation was perhaps worse than the hippies who came afterwards. At least the hippies seemed to be more honest and open about their true feelings.

Much to my surprise, when I went through registration they insisted that all Freshmen were required to take certain courses regardless of their major. They did not believe me when I explained that art majors would only need to learn how to draw and paint. I lost the argument (Boy, did I feel dumb!) and they saddled me with several classes which would require study and library work. I quickly pulled my torn sweat-shirt over my exposed T-shirt and walked out as though I expected to succeed.

In addition to the basic art requirements I took French, History and English Literature. I was able to drift through French with very little effort and to convince the professor that I knew enough French to get a relatively good grade ("What a dumb professor," I thought. "Imagine giving a good grade to a dumb-dumb!"). History and English were different. We had to do some research in the big building with all those books and write a paper.

The university library was much worse than anything I had ever seen in high school. It was several stories high with books on every floor. The first floor had a large room full of little boxes packed with cards. On each card there was the name of an author and the title of a book. We were expected to find the books we wanted without even knowing which books we were looking for.

"How I wish my big brother were here," I cried quietly to myself. "He would be able to find the books and do the reports easily."

I would not dare ask anyone how to find the books I needed. They might see my dumb-dumb T-shirt! I somehow managed to find something and to write some words in a folder in such a way as to have the appearance of a research paper. I honestly do not remember how I was able to get through that first year with grades which were half decent. I do know that I never went back to that library. It was too intimidating.

As the end of the second term drew near, some of my friends began to talk about the military service.

"They will give you some tests to find out what you are capable of doing," I overheard, "then they will train you in that field."

That sounded good to me. Surely "Uncle Sam" would be able

to find a place for me to fit in. With his training program I would certainly be able to learn how to do something useful. Besides, I had also heard that their token master would never cut anyone off from the community unless he did something really bad. I did not expect to get many promotions, but I knew that I was not bad—only dumb. The decision was made. I joined the United States Air Force that summer. I saw myself as becoming part of one of the biggest and most secure treehouses in the jungle.

After a few weeks of basic training at Lackland Air Force Base, in San Antonio, Texas, we were given a battery of tests. While we were waiting for the results of the testing, I was having nightmares about spending the rest of my life in the Air Force peeling potatoes. I was sure that all the other fellows would go on to exciting careers and I would be left behind.

When the results of those tests came back I was sure there had been some kind of mistake. They were going to ship me off to electronics school at Keesler Air Force Base in Biloxi, Mississippi. I could not add or subtract, much less work with the higher math formulas. I had bluffed my way through High School but I knew this would be different. My T-shirt was about to be exposed. There was nothing I could do to stop it. If I drew attention to the mistake, they would see I was dumb. If I went on to the school it would soon become even more evident. I decided to take a chance on bluffing my way through school.

In about two weeks I found myself in a military classroom studying electronics. I was becoming a "hero" of the electronics technician variety. I could not believe it.

"A dumb-dumb in electronics school," I thought. "What is the U.S.A.F. coming to?"

The continual yelling of the sergeant kept me from retreating into my imagination. I was not sure what they would do to me if they caught me "drawing" in my "closet" so I studied. I did not know what else to do. The excitement of learning how those mysterious radar sets worked also helped keep me in the outside world.

After several weeks in the classroom we began to get reports on our progress. According to the reports I was doing very well, much to my amazement. In fact I was doing better than most of the fellows who were with me in the class.

"How can this be?" I asked myself. "How can a dumb-dumb do well in electronics school?" I assumed there must be some mistake in the records or this must be an exceptionally dumb class. Of course, I told no one what I was thinking. I acted as though I expected to do well. I had found a new way to cover my T-shirt. I pretended to be smart.

Our first break came and I had gone to the beach just outside Biloxi. The question of identity was pressing its way to the surface. Something very real seemed to be happening, and I did not know what to do with it.

"Could it be that I am not really dumb?" That possibility almost swept me off my feet. But there was something peaceful about the movement of the sand beneath the surface of the incoming tide. "I might have a place in this jungle after all..." The pleasant thoughts continued to flow in with the tide. I am not sure how long I was standing still there in the surf. It was as though time had been suspended at high tide; there was no movement, only the sense of being "present." I was a person.

The tide began to change, the breeze was increasing and I suddenly became aware that it was getting late. It was time for me to return to the base. I felt the sand shifting under my feet as a thousand little particles scampered back into hiding—back into the security of the deep—as though they were frightened by the light and the rising wind.

The air began to chill and I suddenly realized that I was walking on the beach with my T-shirt exposed. "Who do you think you are?" The accusing voice came from the closet. "Your dumb-dumb credentials have been stamped and verified in every stage of your life. You are dumb, and you know it. Come back to reality."

So I came back to reality; or did I just come out of reality back into my make-believe world? Which was real, the beach or the base? How could I know? Besides, the "spell" had been broken and I could not pursue the matter anyway. Even if I could pursue it, time would not allow it. I had to get back.

I was inwardly puzzled for several weeks as the sense of "becoming" remained with me. As the reality of that experience drifted farther into the past, I finally concluded that I must be some sort of dumb-dumb who was clever enough to bluff the teachers into thinking that I knew more than I really did. After all my teachers in grammar school, junior high and high school had all tried to convince me that I was smarter than I thought I was.

The more I thought about it, the more it began to make sense. Somehow the cover-up techniques which I had developed were so effective that no one knew how dumb I was, except me. I was actually able to convince people that I understood things which no dumb-dumb could possibly understand.

"Now that is an ability which could prove to be useful in the jungle," I thought. When I considered that more seriously, however, it was obvious I would not be able to do that consistently. Eventually I would get caught.

"Probably I have just had some lucky breaks," I heard myself speaking almost audibly. "All that thinking on the beach was probably nothing more than tension vaporizing into wishful imaginations."

Graduation day finally came at Keesler. We were all awarded our certificates and assigned to various places throughout the world. My assignment was to Japan. I had heard about that place. One could buy cameras and watches, even tailored suits, for almost nothing. Here was my chance to collect a bunch of things to put on my shelves when I came back to the states. People would think I was really successful.

I put on my new "Electronic Hero" shirt, boarded the airplane, and off I went "into the wild blue yonder."

"Me, an electronics technician!" Boy, was I excited.

The experience of my first few weeks in Japan was a real let-down. My assignment was to an Air Force base near Tokyo, but I had to stay in a transit barrack until the official orders caught up with me. The crew I had been assigned to did not know I was coming. So I waited. There was nothing to do, and I was not allowed off base. I did not have a friend within six thousand miles.

I was alone, and I was lonely.

I smoked over two packs of cigarettes a day during that time. That did not help, but at least it kept me occupied. Everyone else was coming in one day and leaving the next. No one was even interested in a game of cards. The worst thing of all was that no one noticed my new "Hero" shirt. They were all too busy polishing their own badges.

The orders finally arrived and I was moved to Yokota Air Force Base. When I reported for duty, however, another problem developed. Since my work would be in an area where Top Secret information was available, I would need a security clearance. While they were waiting for their detectives to check out my history and background, they assigned me to a little shop that repaired broken radar equipment.

Most of the units they asked me to work on looked like they had been manufactured in the stone age—out of stone! I had not seen anything like that during my training at Keesler. The old "how and why" syndrome began to return with a new dimension. Not only did I want to know how and why before starting to work, I also needed to know what the unit was supposed to do when I was finished with it.

I felt as though one of the buttons on my "Hero" shirt had dropped off. Just as my T-shirt was about to be exposed, one of the airmen working there took me aside and explained the rules of the Air Force game.

"The rules are very simple," he said. "If anyone does his work too well it makes the rest of the group look bad. As a penalty for doing your work well, your nose will turn brown; you become a marked man and will be cut off from the group."

To be part of the "in" group was important to me, and I certainly did not want my nose to turn brown. So I relaxed, sewed on my button and went back to work. This was a very comfortable situation for me. I could work slowly, think carefully about the hows and whys, even make a few mistakes. Everyone would think I was just playing the game well. If I did something dumb I could simply recall that the "rules" would not allow me to do too well anyway. I got myself a new shirt, sewed on the word "Inconspicuous", and joined the ranks of the complacent.

As soon as my security clearance came through, I settled into my new position in the biggest treehouse in the jungle, Uncle Sam's military services. I had no way of knowing that this would not be a permanent hide-out for me. It was my intention to become a career man in the U.S. Air Force. Uncle Sam was becoming a security symbol for me in the sense that I could look to him in the way I had once looked at my dad, many years earlier, and know everything would be okay.

There in the "Big Treehouse" I knew what was expected of me and I knew how to do it. Most of all I felt free to make a few mistakes. Everyone would think I was just keeping my nose clean.

The word which had been planted within my heart as a young boy, the word which had convinced me I was dumb, was no longer a conscious influence after this. Actually it had not been a conscious issue for quite some time (perhaps it had never been fully conscious). Under its influence, however, I had learned to fear rejection and to order my behavior in such a way as to be accepted (at least superficially).

If I had selected the "success" crowd as "my people" the situation would have been different. I would have been willing to face the "brown-nose" accusations in order to be "in" with the community of the successful. But, in either case, the dynamic behind the behavior would have been a striving for acceptance and a fear of rejection. The fact that it is a different group whose acceptance is desired does not change the reality of what is happening on the level of the unconscious images.

Even at this stage, then, the fear of separation continues to creep in with its death trap. The power of Sheol is so subtle in its deception. Driven to act in such a way as to avoid separation, we end up having only superficial relationships (which is only another form of separation). One who has the potential of becoming more than he is presently (which probably includes almost all of us) is often fearful of becoming what he **could** be lest he experience separation from the group he is presently identified with.

On the other hand, there are those who are driven to gain acceptance among the next higher group. No matter how successful one becomes, it seems there is always someone "out there somewhere" who is doing better. The tendency is to feel that one has still not arrived and to increase ones efforts to be a part of the community of the successful. In either case, whether driven to remain or driven to climb up, the relationships are not real because they are based on doing, not being.

Even those who choose to be in the ranks of the complacent cannot remain there long without becoming frustrated. Sooner or later the drive to become what one is capable of being will return and the striving to achieve will continue. Few are willing to wander in the wilderness of nonachievement for very long, at least not while they still have the vigor of youth within them. While the comfort of complacency does provide a measure of rest, the pressure of the drive for outward evidence of self-worth will continue to build. It will eventually erupt into striving, as long as there remains any vestige of caring about oneself.

For some, the "volcano" of striving for more is in a constant state of eruption. There are businessmen, for example, who are unable to relax and be with their families and friends because they are striving to be in the next highest income bracket. The extra money itself is often not the real motivating factor. They desire recognition and acceptance within a certain group which they consider to be one step higher. The problem is, when they gain that recognition and become one of that group, there is always another higher plateau to which they now desire to climb. They are always in limbo between two groups, being a part of neither. In striving for a sense of belonging to a higher group they have no sense of belonging to any group.

The writer of Ecclesiastes was not overstating the case when he said:

Then I saw that all toil and all skill in work come from a man's envy of his neighbor. This also is vanity and striving after wind...Again, I saw vanity under the sun: a person who has no one, either son or brother, yet there is no end to all his toil, and his eyes are never satisfied with riches, so that he never asks,

"For whom am I toiling and depriving myself of pleasure?" This also is vanity and an unhappy business. (Ecc. 4:4,7,8)

Many people are not able to stop pressing for the "more" long enough to ask themselves why. The answer (which they secretly "know") is too difficult to face. It is too painful to consider the possibility that, apart from productivity, they have no self-worth, no right to belong.

In all our striving to do our work (when we are in that "mode"), we often hide behind high-sounding cliches: "If a job is not worth doing well, it is not worth doing at all." This is true enough, but the question we are raising here is whether we are really working toward improvement in methods and efficiency with the "job well done" as our primary motive, or do we desire the better product or more efficient method as some external proof or symbol of our acceptability? Are we really striving to belong because we inwardly (on the level of self-image) think we have no right to belong?

Sometimes we use our families as an excuse for the longer hours and extra energy needed for acceptance in the "success" crowd. If our families were the real issue, however, would we not want to have those extra hours for them? Would we not desire to conserve our energies for the time we have with them? But spending the extra hours and expending the extra energy, we deprive those for whom we **say** we are working of the things they need above all else—fatherhood, motherhood and friendship.

The man who, under the guise of doing it for his wife, depriving himself of time to be with her in order to achieve a higher level of success, seldom asks himself why he does this. The woman who, under the guise of doing it for her children, depriving herself of family time to be more involved in the community, seldom asks herself why she is depriving herself of time with her children. The reason we seldom ask is because we secretly know the answer. We are striving after wind. It is painful to become aware of the fact that we are driven by a dynamic within ourselves over which we have little control. We feel as though we are caught on some sort of carousel which will not stop for us to get off. Life has aptly been called a rat race. We all run over one another, or ignore one another, as we chase after our own piece of cheese.

In **longing** to belong we give evidence that we do not feel we **do** belong. One does not long for what he knows he has. In **striving** to have external proof of our right to belong we give evidence that we inwardly **doubt** our right to belong. This is obviously true when our striving takes the form of super-achievement. We are trying to appear acceptable in the community of the successful. It is just as true, though less obvious, when our striving takes the form of under-achievement. In this case we are trying to appear acceptable in the ranks of the complacent.

In either case there is another issue which will arise sooner or later for those who are courageous enough to grant it conscious awareness. We speak here of the question, "Would anyone out there accept me if they knew what I was hiding? Can anyone love me just for me, without the external cover of performance or possessions?" When this question is allowed to surface, even without full consciousness, it brings with it a new and unexpected dynamic. We begin to do things specifically designed to **expose** what we consider to be our real inner nature.

Two very different kinds of behavior patterns are discernable at this point. Remembering the diagram in chapter one, we offer it here again with additions representing these behavior patterns (see Fig. #2). On the one hand there is behavior which is intended to **cover up** the poor self-image. On this level are those things which we do and say to avoid exposing our T-shirts. Our discussion to this point has concentrated on this kind of behavior.

On the other hand there is behavior which is designed intentionally (though perhaps unconsciously) to **expose** the T-shirt. The purpose is to discover someone out there who can accept us in spite of how "dumb" we are. We are seldom conscious of this motivation. Even to ourselves we seem to do "dumb" things (or to fail in some way) for no apparent reason. After we do or say those things we step back and ask ourselves, "Why would I do a dumb thing like that?" Or we simply try to give some (equally dumb) excuse for our behavior. And we are not really surprised when people reject us for those things, because we have already rejected ourselves.

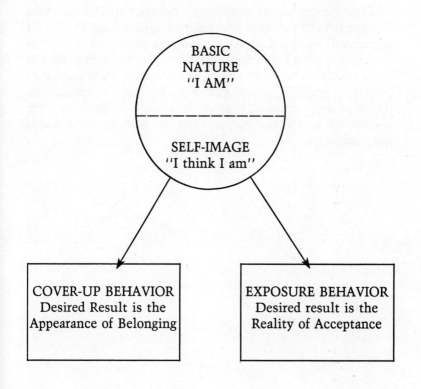

FIGURE #2

TWO KINDS OF BEHAVIOR

This phenomenon of "exposure" behavior will be discussed in more detail later. It is now time to raise a more significant question: Is there a way out? Is there any possibility of coming to a place of being the kind of person who has freedom to express the **reality** of who he or she **is, deep within,** with no fear of embarrassment? The **cover-up** produces deceptive **acceptance** and the **exposure** produces obvious rejection. Is there another alternative? It is to this question that we turn our attention in the next chapter.

5

VENETIAN BLINDS

Light Dispels Darkness

I remember well those days in Japan. After working through the frustrations of the first few weeks, I became very comfortable in my position there. My responsibilities were clearly defined and I enjoyed what I was doing. I was even considering a permanent career in the Air Force. My superiors were satisfied with my work and encouraged me regularly. I was even up for a promotion. Everything seemed right, except I was still uncomfortable within myself.

This inner turmoil was brought to the surface when a sergeant from a different crew came to invite me to go to church with him. The military always made the "religious preference" list available to the various church groups on base. The sergeant was a member of the same religious group which I had grown up in and he had taken my name from that list. Because of my religious training I felt I **ought** to go, so I agreed. When Sunday morning came, however, I became aware that I did not **want** to go. So I stayed in the barrack.

"What has church ever done for me?" I thought. "All they

ever do is just sing the same old songs and listen to the same old sermons.''

I had a Bible but I never read it. There were two reasons: first, because I did not enjoy reading anything (reading reminded me of libraries), and second, because I knew that if I did read that particular book it would remind me of all the "oughts" in my life. I wanted to be a part of the crowd that was having a good time. I seldom stopped to notice that when I was having a good time, I was not really having a good time. No one else did either. The fact is that none of us ever stopped having "fun" long enough to notice anything. We were too busy pretending to be busy so we would not **have** to notice.

Most of the time I tried to stay out of my "closet" as well. The place of quiet meditation and secret adventures was no longer quiet, and it was no longer exciting. When I went in there I was only reminded of the "oughts" and "ought-nots" which I was no longer living by. The closet had become a place of condemnation rather than a place of rest and peace. Time spent in there was no longer productive in any sense of the word. I could no longer receive even imaginary acceptance by retreating.

As long as I was able to keep myself distracted by activity at work or by "noise" in recreation I could avoid the accusing voices which were constantly trying to belch forth from the closet. With busy-ness and hyperactivity I did not have to face either my pretense (trying to convince myself that my life style was fulfilling) or my conscience (knowing that things were not right within). Inwardly I was much like a shrimp. When I tried to go to the depths to avoid the birds, the big fish would tear me to pieces. When I tried to surface to avoid the big fish, the birds would pick me apart. So I continued to seek new and more exciting distractions.

I had made a commitment to Jesus as a child. An evangelist had come to our church in Carlsbad, New Mexico, and preached for two weeks. "Running the Race" was the title of the sermon which caught my attention. I can still remember the large chart he had drawn on a white sheet and displayed before the congregation. The picture was of an arena in which various kinds of runners were illustrated at different points on the "track" of life. At the end was a big golden crown for those who finished the race.

He captured my imagination with his illustrations. The seed had been planted and was germinating even as he spoke. In my childhood devotion I wanted to please Jesus.

"To please Him," the preacher said, "you must be baptized." Then he read some Bible verses.

I went forward and was immersed in water that night. I can still remember the congregation singing, "Oh Happy Day, When Jesus Washed my Sins Away." When I came up out of the water I knew that something very real had happened. They said that I had become a new creature, but I did not have any idea what that meant. I only knew that there was something very peaceful deep within the inner closet.

That had been many years earlier. My closet had long since become so cluttered with many voices clambering for attention that I had forgotten the inner stillness which had come with such assurance. Even if I had remembered, I probably would not have chosen to listen for that voice of stillness at that time. I was too busy finding out what "life" had to offer.

The sergeant continued to come by and ask why I was not coming to church, and I continued to make excuses. Every time he came around I would be reminded of the contrast between what I knew to be "right" and what I was actually doing. The inner conflict would return with new force.

"Maybe I should try to quit smoking before I start going back to church," I excused myself, "then perhaps I would feel like I belong there."

I honestly tried to quit several times. One time I was successful for three whole weeks. I made a card to help remind me I was quitting. To provide adequate motivation, I drew a stairway on the card with "heaven" at the top and "hell" at the bottom. "Each cigarette I smoke will be a step downward," I told myself as I put the card in my pocket to replace the cancer sticks. It did not occur to me at that time that I had not provided any means by which I might take steps upward.

That worked very well for about three weeks. Then one of my "friends" offered me a drag, and I accepted it. There I was on my way down. I was not really surprised. I suppose I really expected to fail. For a short time I was faithful to keep a record of my smokes on the card. When it became clear what was happening, I did the only sensible thing—I threw away the card and began looking for more exciting diversions.

One of the things which kept me distracted was the weekend trips out into the Japanese countryside. My motorcycle took me into many areas where very few Americans ever went. I learned enough of the language to get by among the people. These excursions took me to many ancient shrines and various points of historical and cultural interest. The country was beautiful and the people were kind and receptive. But I was running.

At times I felt as though I were out there looking for something I had lost, or misplaced, or maybe never had. "That experience on the beach in Mississippi seemed so real," I thought. "If only I could recapture that timeless moment and continue my search for the real me." But those moments cannot be created by man. They come and go as they please.

At other times it seemed I was running away from something, or someone. I certainly did not want to face the reality of "Dumb-Dumb" in his present life style. I had myself well covered as far as the outsiders were concerned. Many were probably envious of the freedom that I appeared to have. But I knew what was on the inside, at least I thought I did. I was afraid to look too closely at my inner condition, it might be even worse than I knew. So I continued to look at the countryside. That was not as likely to expose me.

The moment of reality came one morning after I had been on duty as a night watchman. It was later than I would normally rise but earlier than I had anticipated. The night shift had not been difficult and I had rested well. I had left the venetian blinds partly open as I had gone to bed in the middle of the night. When I awoke, the sun was shining in and filling the room with light. Everything was radiant with the promise of a good day, and so it was to be.

The barracks at Yokota A.F.B. were not of the open bay variety. They had been partitioned off into a long hallway with semi-private sleeping quarters on either side. Each room held from two to six bunks with adequate locker space and a study desk. I was one of the more fortunate airmen who had to share a room with only one other person. For all practical purposes I had the room all to myself. My roommate was always "out with the boys" when he was not on duty. At this particular time he was on a three day pass. I knew he would not be around.

Since I had been on guard duty the night before, I was allowed to post a "Day Sleeper" sign on my door. Unlike some other barracks, that sign was respected in our area. That was a welcome assurance for me on that particular morning. The identity questions were beginning to rise again.

"What am I becoming?" The question greeted me as my eyelids broke to make a way for the morning light.

I got dressed and sat at the reading desk looking out the window. I saw several children gathering for their swimming lessons at the pool across the street. They were running, jumping, laughing. Life seemed so simple for them.

"If only I could be like a little child again," I sighed. But I knew one could never go back. I wondered if it would really be desirable to be little again anyway. What possible advantage could there be in that? I would only have to grow up again, and there was no guarantee things would be any better the second time through.

Their swimming instructor arrived and the sound of their laughter frittered away into the dressing rooms. I lit a cigarette and waited, though I honestly did not know what I was waiting for. If you had asked me then, I probably would not have even known that I **was** waiting. I was just staring. The silent stillness returned.

"Perhaps I will take a ride on my motorcycle," I thought. "It is a nice day for that sort of thing."

It was a pleasant thought, but I was immediately apprehended by the silence. There would be no diversions or distractions that day. Something, or someone, was calling, wooing from the other side of stillness. I did not understand what was happening. Even if I had known that the Lord was approaching, I would not have known what to do. In fact, I probably would have run away because I did not yet know of His loving forgiveness. I would have expected Him to condemn me.

The thought of His coming would not have occurred to me anyway. I was raised to be very suspicious of people who claimed to have actually met the Lord. Anyone who said that he had heard from or spoken to the Lord was either intentionally deceiving people or he was a candidate for the "funny farm" where the authorities put such people. Nothing in my background or training had prepared me to expect, or even to anticipate, what was about to happen.

I left the cigarette in the ash tray and went to check the door. It was locked. For some reason I needed to know that. As I returned and saw the smoke rising from the cigarette, I thought, "I do not need that right now." So I doused it and lay down on my bunk. Folding my hands on my chest, I looked up at the ceiling. My thoughts were racing back and forth through the various experiences that had come my way during the past few months. I did not know what else to do. I could not withdraw, being captivated by the reality of the moment, nor could I approach. So I waited.

Suddenly I was aware that someone was in the room with me. He had not come in, He was just there. I did not see Him, but His presence filled the room. The "presence" was so real to me that I lifted my hands to embrace Him. I knew it was the Lord. I do not know how I knew, I just knew. And I knew that He loved me and accepted me as I was, even though He knew all about me. The room was filled with what can only be described as liquid love. As I had been immersed in water as a child, I was there being immersed in His love. He who is LOVE had come to me in that place.

None of my fantasies in the closet had ever been like this. This was real. I was fully aware of the natural surroundings in the room; but His presence was far more real than all that. I had come face to face with a reality which was far beyond anything which is normally called real. It was as though the One who lives on the other side of the closet had rent the veil and come to be with me on this side. Or perhaps He had taken me with Him beyond the veil. This much I know: He was there and He loved me with an everlasting love.

Something within me had come of age. The seed which had germinated within me as a boy was breaking forth from the soil and reaching for the sky—and beyond. The "me" inside was very much alive. That life in me was quickened by the realization and acknowledgement that the "Beloved of Heaven" had received me. He was well aware of my fears and my failures, He knew all about those things which I was able to hide from others. But he received me—He loved me just as I was.

I was not alone, and I was not lonely. As I lay there on my bunk looking up at my raised hands, it occurred to me how dumb that would appear to anyone who was not a part of the experience. But I would not have been embarrassed if someone had been watching because I knew it was not dumb. Being received of the Lord had dispelled all fear of rejection. Everything seemed so right, it was real, it was okay. Lowering my hands to my chest again, I continued to drink of His presence. With each inhaling breath I was receiving love, joy and peace. With each exhaling breath I was being relieved of insecurity, unworthiness and inadequacy. Feelings of guilt and defilement were being washed away in the flood. Later I wrote these words:

Then there was evening,
Then there was morning.
>When silent streams of sunlight
>>seeping through the windowshades
>>to greet emerging consciousness
>Have put to flight the Savage
>Shadows of the Cloven Hoof,
Then breaks Eternal Day.

The **sense** of His presence slowly faded. From that day to this, however, I have known that He is real and that He is always "there" with His love. There was a residue remaining deep within, an abiding presence which would soon be leading me into experiences and accomplishments which I would never have believed possible for me. I spent the rest of the day enjoying the newness of what I felt inside. The next Sunday I was in church, not because of any sense of obligation; I wanted to be there.

During the next few weeks there was a particularly visible sign of the new freedom I was experiencing. I left some cigarettes in the drawer of the desk and never went back to them. One day I suddenly realized that my roommate had smoked them all. This time it was not a decision on my part to quit smoking. It just happened. Somehow all the desire for nicotine had been taken away. I did not do that; it was done **to** me. I had been set free— even without asking. The "how" and "why" of it all was beyond me but I did not care; I was free.

That which had come of age in me at that time was not a product of the seed of Adam. The adamic nature has nothing within itself which is capable of producing this kind of change. External activity (such as smoking) might be conquered by human effort, but the change of which we speak here is much deeper. What is indicated is not a tune-up for the old man (i.e., the adamic nature), not even a complete overhaul. We speak of the **creation** of a **new man in Christ.** As we mentioned in the "Introduction", the self which is in need of improvement is not adequate to the task. The help which man needs must come from beyond man. Any do-it-yourself kit for self-improvement is doomed to failure. Mere improvement is not the creation of a new nature. Some adjustments and additions to our diagram will be helpful in explaining this concept (see Fig. #3).

Jesus said to Nicodemus, "That which is born of flesh is flesh, and that which is born of Spirit is spirit. Do not marvel that I said to you, 'You must be born anew' " (Jn. 3:6,7). Paul exhorted the Ephesians, "Put off your old nature which belongs to your former manner of life and is corrupt through deceitful lusts, and be renewed in the spirit of your minds, and put on the new nature, created in the likeness of God in true righteousness and holiness" (Eph. 4:22-24). As the old nature is related to the **seed of generation,** so the new nature is related to the **seed of regeneration.** As the "old man" is a **product of the flesh,** so the

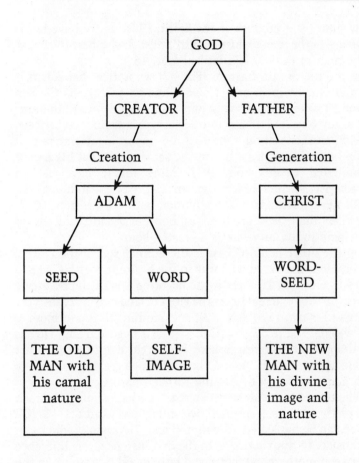

FIGURE #3

TWO KINDS OF GENERATION

"new man" is a **product of the Spirit.** "Just as we have borne the image of the man of dust (Adam), we shall also bear the image of the man of heaven (Christ)" (I Cor. 15:49).

At the top of our diagram (Fig. #3) we notice that Adam is a son of God by creation (Lk. 3:38) and that Christ is the Son of God by generation. Discussions about regeneration, or being born again, often fail to take into account this distinction between creation and generation. One does not impart his nature to that which he builds, at least not in the same sense that his nature is imparted to his son. A building might have certain characteristics which reflect the personality of the architect, but it will never participate in his human nature—it is a building. Likewise, man as man (i.e., as born of Adam) will never participate in divinity—he is a created being.

On the other hand, Christ is the eternal Son of the eternal Father. He is the Word who was in the beginning with God and who was God (Jn. 1:1). He is the begotten Son of the begetting Father (Jn. 1:14). "He reflects the glory of God and bears the very stamp of his nature" (Heb. 1:3), and "in him all the fullness of God was pleased to dwell" (Col. 1:19). As Begotten Son, He has two things which interest us here. He has the **nature** of the Father and He has within His "loins" the **seed** which is able to reproduce itself and produce in others the Father's nature.

When Jesus spoke of the new birth, Nicodemus misunderstood Him on two counts. Jesus used two ambiguous words: (1) "born" (which can be translated "begotten") and (2) "again" (which can be translated "from above"). In the first instance, the difference is between **motherhood** (born) and **fatherhood** (begotten). In the second, the difference is between **repetition** (again) and **origin** or source (from above). Nicodemus betrayed his lack of understanding by his question, "How can a man be born when he is old? Can he enter a second time (repetition) into his mother's womb (motherhood) and be born?"

First of all, with reference to the question of motherhood or fatherhood, it is clear from the whole of John's Gospel that the fatherhood of God is one of the major ideas which John is trying to present. The purpose of the fatherhood theme is to draw attention to the fact that the nature of a father is reproduced in his son. One's nature is determined by the seed of his generation. As wheat produces wheat and corn produces corn, so pig seed produces pig nature and human seed produces human nature. In the thinking of biblical man, the "mother's womb" is the environment in which the seed is given opportunity to develop. The conditions within that environment will certainly influence that development. But if the seed is from a pig, the offspring will be a pig, and if the seed is from a human, the offspring will be a human.

Second, with reference to the question of repetition or origin, what possible advantage could there be in being born a second time if there is no more than a mere repetition? Even if it were possible to repeat the "mother's womb" experience, a pig would still be "pig" and a human would still be "human." Nicodemus might not have been Nicodemus (if he were able to part from his mother a second time); he might have been given another name and he might have even developed differently, but he would have still been human. Flesh (human nature apart from God) produces flesh. Those things in our lives which cause us to be aware of our need for basic changes have come to us through our human generation. There was something fundamentally wrong in the first birth. Why go through that a second time? The self-centered nature of Adam can only reproduce after its kind.

A study of the whole of John's Gospel will also reveal that the concept of origin, "from above", plays a major role in the development of his theme. The phrase "down from heaven" appears seven times in Jesus' teaching on the bread of life (ch. 6), and the concept appears many more times. The idea of Jesus' being "sent" from God is in almost every teaching. The tendency is to limit the application of this idea of fatherhood and sonship to Jesus and thereby to miss the main point of the Gospel. "But to all who receive him, who believed in his name, he gave power to become children of God; who were born, not of blood nor of the will of the flesh nor of the will of man, but of God" (1:12,13). If one is born of God, that birth is clearly "from above." Jesus was trying to tell Nicodemus that he must be born of God and thereby receive God's nature.

Peter also addressed himself to this theme, although he developed it in a different way. He began by reminding us that "we have been born anew to a living hope through the resurrection of Jesus Christ from the dead" (I Pet. 1:3). It is true that Peter used a word which means "again" in the sense of a second time. But he gave precise definition to this "second time" when he said, "You have been born anew, not of perishable seed but of imperishable, through the living and abiding word of God" (1:23). Here he made it abundantly clear that this "second time" is an experience fundamentally different from the first time. It is not a mere repetition of the same thing. The seed of this generation comes from God, not from man. It comes from above.

In response to Nicodemus' question, then, we must answer that it is impossible for man to enter the womb a second time and be born when he is old. Even if he could, however, nothing of eternal significance would be accomplished by that second experience. The birth of which Jesus spoke can never be a result of man's will or man's efforts. Man as **producer** can never **produce** Spirit as **product.** Flesh is flesh and can only produce flesh. "It is the spirit that gives life," Jesus said, "the flesh is of no avail; the words that I have spoken to you are spirit and life" (Jn. 6:63). The seed/word of God is the Word which **is** God and which arrives on the scene as Lord. It is never under the control of man's flesh. Man can only receive it as a miracle.

Having received the miracle of the new birth, we do not immediately become spiritual giants. We do not come into the kingdom of God as mature Christians. As we must grow up physically, so we must grow up spiritually. And as there are struggles in our physical and emotional development, so there will be struggles in our spiritual development. Join me in the next chapter as I share some of my growing pains.

6

OVERCOATS AND ARMORS

Seeking After Certainty

When my time with the Air Force was fulfilled, they flew me back to the United States for a discharge from active service. The desire to continue my career with the military was no longer with me. The changes which had taken place within me while I was in Japan had completely redirected my life. One thing was now very clear to me. I knew I would never be satisfied doing anything other than teaching the Word of God. But it was really more than a question of personal satisfaction; there was a sense of the destiny of a divine calling. I knew I **must** prepare myself to teach.

With a sense of confidence beyond any previous experience, I enrolled at Eastern New Mexico University in Portales, New Mexico. That particular university attracted my attention for several reasons. It had a department of religion and biblical studies which was funded by the various churches in that area. That provided an opportunity to receive an education in the field of my interest at state college prices. The cost of the private schools was prohibitive for me at that time. One of the major factors in this choice, however, was the religious training of my youth.

The church I grew up in taught that we were the only ones who were right. One of the professors in the religion department was "one of us" so I felt safe from the destructive doctrines which I assumed the "others" would be teaching.

My concept of a religious education was very limited at that time. Somehow I thought that the instructors would show me where all the Bible verses are which would prove that we were right. Then I would memorize all the verses with their references. The next step would be to learn how to string the verses together into sermons. Then I would be ready to go out and prove to the whole world that we had all the truth. I was in for some real surprises.

I did relatively well that first year in spite of the trauma of discovering how small my vision of reality was. The more I learned about the historical and cultural background of the Bible, the more I became aware of my ignorance. As I was introduced to the biblical languages it became clear that some of the doctrines of "our" church were a result of straining out the gnats and swallowing camels. Many of our favorite arguments were nothing more than forcing the text to say what we wanted to hear rather than allowing the text to speak for itself. I also learned that most of the questions with which we approached the text had nothing to do with the message the author was trying to convey.

I suppose one reason I was able to live through all that change in such a short time was that I was still naive enough to believe "our people" would be excited to learn the things I was learning and to gain new insights into the scriptures. Surely our people— the people of God who pride themselves in establishing their doctrines on the biblical text—would be open to hear any teaching which was firmly founded on the Scriptures. Surely they would be interested in learning what those Bible verses "really" meant. Why should they not be happy for me to tell them how wrong they had been? I suppose I was as arrogant as I was naive. Fortunately I did not have to face disillusionment on that level until later.

As I continued my education, two dynamics began to operate in my life. One was a deep desire to know and understand what was real and true. Making a break from the "futile ways inherited from your fathers" (I Pet. 1:18) is a difficult and threatening process. It seemed that, with each new thing I learned, a new area was exposed where I had been indoctrinated. Much of what I had believed before entering college was either misleading or contrary to the facts. My confidence in human authority was quickly fading. It became obvious that I must discover truth for myself. I wanted to know how and why rather than merely quoting what others had said.

It was not long before the enormity of the task which I had selected for myself began to swell and overwhelm me. Each time I tried to establish certainty on any given issue I would come face-to-face with several other areas of uncertainty. Each new door I opened in the university led only to another hallway with several doors leading to other hallways and other doors. There was very little of any substance behind any of those doors. There were only more questions. Soon I was lost in the labyrinth of academic pursuit.

It became obvious that the task I had selected was too big for me. I suspect that it was probably a task too large for anyone. I began to look for something, or someone, from which I could derive some sense of direction. I read the philosophers and the psychologists—this was not a part of the degree plan I was following; I just had to know. I read the theologians and the scholars of world religions. I knew there must be some hidden ingredient which I had over-looked. During that time I came to identify with the "preacher" in Ecclesiastes who said, "...in much wisdom is much vexation, and he who increases knowledge increases sorrow" (Ecc. 1:18).

What I had not understood before beginning this journey is that, once you have begun, short of a miracle there is no turning back, at least not this side of insanity. There was not even a guarantee that the road would not itself lead to insanity. During those difficult years I penned this meditation:

Now I Must Know
Looking for guidance
From one who has gone before,
Someone is there in the fog.

Can you help a man lost on his way
And direct him which path he should take?

I'm here where I am,
His reply was so pleasant,
I see no farther ahead.
I have come this far from who knows whence,
From here the path leads who knows whither.
Perhaps I am lost as well.

Then came the whirlwind shifting the fog.
It covered him up, took him away,
Or perhaps it uncovered a path.

How can I know what lies up ahead?
Who am I? Where am I now?
Which way do I go from here?

There's one way to know!

Where I've been there was nothing to keep,
Where I am there is nothing to take,
So now I must go,
For now I must know,
Now I must know,
I must know,
Must know.

I had indeed reached the age of seeking, but I found nothing. I had been well trained to look in the wrong direction for answers. This driving desire for knowledge was beginning to control my life. I had been stung by the Asp of Eden. Having experienced a personal awakening I saw no alternative but to continue seeking after certainty. Never again would I be content to wander in the wilderness of complacency. Even if I had wanted to, I would not have been able. One can never go back. Not really.

The second dynamic which began to operate in my life at that time was related to the first. The more I learned, the more I became aware of how much I did not know. I did something which I suppose many students do. I compared my level of understanding to that of the upper classmen and sometimes even to my professors. Naturally I came up short. It seemed they knew so much. As I became more aware of how much there was to learn and compared that with my relative ignorance, the old "Dumb-Dumb" syndrome began to return.

It returned slowly and subtly, and with it came the impulse to cover-up. The fear of being exposed grew quietly as I became the upper classman. I remembered well the image I had of "upper classmen" and was convinced that I did not measure up, especially since I was now comparing myself to the graduate students. To maintain the "upper classman" image before those who were "under classmen", I began to pretend to know more than I actually knew. This developed so slowly that I did not recognize it for several years. I realize now that the fear of exposure was greater at that time than the desire for integrity. Thus I began to weave the fabric of what was to become a three-piece suit to cover up my dumb-dumb T-shirt. On the front would be written the word "SMART."

The new confidence with which I had returned from Japan had now become a false confidence. The focus of my attention had shifted from the presence of God to my own ability to use big vocabulary words and complex philosophical constructs in such a way as to convince others that I knew what I was talking about. The truth is that I was as confused and insecure in my thinking as anyone. But I was not willing to face that fact at that time. I was too insecure even to face it myself, and I was certainly not willing for anyone else to see what I was hiding from myself.

I can still remember the anxiety with which I approached the day of graduation from college. I had a high grade-point average and was a member of the honor society, but I was not personally convinced those honors were really mine. I knew how much I did not know. As though this were not enough to produce anxiety, I heard stories of students who had received their folder on graduation night only to find a note inside instructing them to see the registrar. They had not completed all the requirements, so they were not given a diploma. I just knew that would happen to me. What would I tell all my friends?

I even had visions of walking across the platform and watching with embarrassment as the dean fumbled around in the stack of folders looking for mine. I could just see him as he finally realized who I was. I could hear him saying, "I do not seem to have your folder here. Apparently my secretary failed to inform you that there was a mistake in the records and you have not yet completed all the requirements for graduation." There I would be with my "Dumb" exposed in public. To make things even worse I had a secret suspicion that the extra course would be something which would be totally beyond my abilities. I feared I would never graduate.

The big day came. I donned the scholar's robe and walked to the platform. The dean called my name, handed me a folder; and I walked off. I would not dare look inside while everyone was watching. They might judge me to be insecure. When sufficiently out of view, I opened the folder and looked inside. Sure enough, there was a diploma inside. The amazing thing was that it had my name on it. I could hardly resist the thought, "What a dumb university. Imagine giving a B.A. degree to a dumb-dumb!"

Now it was legal for me to wear my "Smart" suit in public. I quickly began to parade my knowledge in Sunday schools and church services. I seldom thought of the experience in Japan any more. Without realizing it, I had lost sight of the One who had approached me there and had come to focus my attention on knowledge gained by study. In searching after knowledge and certainty, and striving thereby to cover my low self-esteem, I had been robbed of that fresh flow of life I had once known.

Occasionally I did remember the excitement of those days in Japan and would wonder what had gone wrong. A deep longing would rise up within me. I wanted to return to the simplicity of walking daily in His presence. But "experience" had very little place within the churches of my childhood and training. So I continued to concentrate on doctrine like they did. The wisdom of this world (in spite of the fact that it was applied to Bible and theology) had become a veil over my mind (II Cor. 3:15) to make me insensitive to the presence I had once known.

He was "there", but there was no longer any fellowship or personal communion.

By this time I had become convinced, somehow or other, that the only way to know God was through study. Applying the natural mind to the Scripture seemed to be the right approach but the Scripture was becoming the written code that kills (II Cor. 3:6). I was dying on the vine and did not even know it. The only verses I thought I understood, perhaps the only ones I noticed any more, were those concerning the doctrines which our church considered important. I thought the "written code" was the Old Testament Law and assumed that the phrase, "the Spirit gives life," was speaking of man's logical capacity to wrestle a meaning from Scripture.

I thought that God had somehow lost interest in leading men into all truth (Jn. 16:13) after the close of the first century. That promise was only for the Old Testament prophets and New Testament apostles. For subsequent ages God had given man a book, a mind and simple instructions: "...work out your own salvation with fear and trembling" (Phil. 2:12). So I was trying, and I was dying. I never noticed the next verse, "For God is at work in you, both to will and to do for his good pleasure." If I had noticed, I would not have understood. I had forgotten how to listen to the Spirit while reading the Bible.

Unconsciously I had learned to rely on human wisdom to discern the meaning of the biblical text. Without recognizing it I was also trying to proclaim "the testimony of God in lofty words of wisdom" rather than in the power of God (I Cor. 2:1-5). In those days I considered it a compliment when people said my teaching was over their heads. I never stopped to ask myself how it could legitimately be called "teaching" if no one understood anything. The people were impressed and entertained, but there was no flow of divine life. Many of us were dry and hungry, but we covered our hunger with a cloak of religious jargon and kept ourselves distracted by religious activities. As long as we were able to use the right words and keep ourselves busy doing church work, we could at least convince the others we were satisfied and fulfilled.

The light which I had seen in Japan was being eclipsed by academic training. I knew that God was not dead, as some theologians were saying. I had become convinced, however, that He was not available for personal fellowship apart from intense intellectual effort and strenuous religious activities on the part of man. The memory of His coming to me without my asking, without my knowing, and in the midst of my selfishness now seemed more like a dream. I **knew** it had been real, but it **seemed** like a dream since, in trying so hard, I had not been able to recapture that **sense** of His presence.

Having been programmed to look within the mind for God, I assumed my need was for more intense study habits and a higher level of education. It did not occur to me that I had known Him and walked with Him before I had studied Greek and History. Driven to understand more deeply and driven to cover my T-shirt more completely, I decided to continue my education. I did not know what else to do. I could not turn back. I had to know more. So I enrolled in graduate school.

Meanwhile a young lady entered my life. I had been engaged twice before, but was too insecure to pursue the relationships. Now that I was well-covered with my "Smart" suit, I felt more confident. Her name was Lynda Richards. She had been valedictorian of her graduating class in high school. My "smart" suit was impressed with that. Besides she was deeply concerned for people and was always busy helping others instead of flirting as the other girls did. We joined our hands together and committed ourselves to one another for life. As it turned out, that is one of the smartest things I have ever done. If I had seen her then for all she is, I am sure I would have considered myself unworthy of such a treasure.

I finished all the course work for the master of arts degree shortly after we were married. My first teaching position was at The Victoria College in Victoria, Texas. The "Bible Chair" was an arrangement where the church paid my salary and the school gave college credit for the Bible courses taught on campus. In that position I became increasingly aware of my inadequacies. The students showed much excitement over the new insights they were receiving, but I felt very insecure each time someone raised a hand to ask a question.

"What if I do not know the answer?" I would inwardly gasp, "My 'Smart' suit will fall open and my T-shirt will be exposed!"

After two years of teaching, I finally finished writing my thesis and received the M.A. degree from Eastern New Mexico University. I saw my graduate degree as a big thick camel's hair overcoat with "DOUBLE-SMART" written on the front. I thought that would help with my insecurities in the classroom. But the feelings were actually intensified because now I was expected to know even more. There would no longer be any excuse for not knowing the answers to the questions the students would ask.

Some students seemed to have an ability to sense which questions would threaten the teacher most. Inevitably, those questions were bound to come up in class. When they did I would simply make up answers with big words and high sounding phrases as I pulled my "DOUBLE-SMART" overcoat tightly around my neck. One more year of that was all I could handle. I had to continue my education. So I made plans to attend The University of Texas at Austin. I had to go for the "big one."

"I will get myself a Ph.D. in the Hebrew language," I thought. "No one will be able to see through that."

I saw myself putting on metal armor, about an inch thick, with a helmet. Everything would be totally covered and it would not fall open when students asked difficult questions. The other dynamic was also still present. I thought I might be able to discover the element which was missing in my devotional life if I could just read the biblical text in the original languages. I was setting myself up for another big disillusionment.

This turned out to be the most intensive study I had ever been exposed to; but I expected that. After learning modern Israeli Hebrew, we attended several classes in which the professors taught in Hebrew; no English was spoken. We studied every stage of the language, from the ancient biblical text to the Mishna, and from Moshe Ben-Maimon to Agnon. Then we were introduced to the cognate languages: Aramaic, Arabic, Akkadian and Ugaritic. I was beginning to wear my armored vest long before I graduated. I was a Ph.D. candidate! I was really impressed with myself.

Insecurity and cover-up were not the only motives for continuing. I still had a deep hunger for knowing God and touching reality as I had done once upon a time. As mentioned earlier, through the education process I had come to equate the intensive study of religious questions with seeking after God. During those years at Austin I was beginning to wonder whether He could be known at all. I never doubted that I had been approached by Him in Japan; that was too real to deny. But every attempt to pursue Him would only lead into another blind alley. I knew He was "there"; I just did not know how to find Him.

The unequivocal knowledge that He was there, somewhere, drove me to continue my search. My plans were to begin work on another Ph.D. as soon as I finished the one in Hebrew studies. If God had not intervened, I would have pursued one degree after another. My contribution to society would have been a series of articles in the academic journals which gather dust in the libraries and frighten the little "dumb-dumbs" who come to college to hide. My life would have been spent trying to find answers to questions which few people ever ask, answers which would not have made the slightest difference in the quality of anyone's life. But God would not have it so.

While finishing the final semester of course work at Austin and planning the dissertation I would be writing the following year, I received notification that my name had been "accidentally" left off the list of those who would be receiving financial aid from the government for post-graduate studies. At the same time a letter came offering me a teaching position at Eastern New Mexico University where I had been a student. As it turned out, I would have received the government grant anyway. But I did not know that until I had already committed myself to teach in New Mexico.

I had come a long way since those Air Force days and had learned many things on the journey. But nothing I had learned could compare with what was waiting for me in my new assignment. I had come through the age of seeking without seeing and was about to enter the age of seeing. Naturally, I did not know that yet. I was excited to get back into teaching. That was my calling, and I knew it.

One thing is apparent as I look back at those years of seeking and striving. The **word** which is implanted within the heart of a child has tremendous formative influence long after it is consciously forgotten. Even in the face of contrary evidence, I was still under the power of the word "dumb." It is not within man to effectively believe against the word of his youth. We have already noticed that, even if one is out to disprove that word, the word is still in a position of power and influence over his behavior. Here the "power of Sheol" works through the poor self-image to convince us that we **"have not"**, no matter how much we **have,** and that we **"can not"**, no matter how well we **do.** Under the influence of this power we continue to strive for more and we seldom ask why.

When we noticed this in chapter three, our attention was focused on the superficial relationships which come from the cover-up. In our next chapter we plan to begin to show the way out. Here our desire is to give more exposure to the drive itself as it is manifested in various situations.

A young man, for example, may judge himself to be a failure because of the "word" he received as a child. Two dynamics keep him in constant tension. On the one hand there is the conscious **feeling** that he **should** be able to do **better** (no matter how well he is doing) since he was always told that he **could** do better if he tried. On the other hand there is the unconscious **knowing** that he **can not** do better (no matter how hard he tries) since he was always criticized even when he gave it his best effort.

Remembering that there are many forms of "wealth" for which man may strive, we can see this power working in many areas. No matter how much evidence one has that he is "successful" (whatever that may mean in any given situation), he knows that his T-shirt reads "FAILURE." One can always find some standard by which to compare himself. If he is making

$1,000 a month, he compares himself to one who makes $1,500. When he gets a raise, he compares himself to one making $2,000 and so on.

The worker who continually strives for a raise in pay may not actually need more money. Everyone can **use** more money, but the desire for more is not necessarily an indication of a financial need. The "raise" may have become a symbol of acceptance from the boss who is no more than a father figure in the worker's personal striving for his father's acceptance. Even when the raise comes in this kind of situation, it is never enough to convince the worker of his acceptance because the lack of approval is coming from within himself. When one secretly disapproves of himself, he can seldom be convinced that another has really accepted him.

Turning now to a different form of wealth; there are attractive girls who think of themselves as ugly. Often the presence of excessive make-up is an attempted cover-up (literally) of the fact that the girl believes she is unattractive. This is also a subtle and deceptive power. No matter how beautiful the girl may be, and in spite of compliments and attention, she still feels ugly. She can never really see herself as pretty because she "knows" what she has covered up. She is driven to find more effective make-up techniques and to buy new, hopefully more attractive, clothes for people to look at. She cannot bear the thought of others seeing her as she "really" is.

How many are climbing social ladders because they feel unworthy and unaccepted? How many are scholars because they feel dumb? Are there professional football players who are on the field because they are trying to convince themselves that they are tough? What about the meticulously clean housekeeper; is she trying to prove to someone that she is not sloppy? Does she actually think that someone will reject her if they find a spot on her furniture? Or under it?

These questions may never have answers. The statistics may never be available. As we ask, however, the deceptive devices of Sheol are exposed. First we become convinced that we are inferior in one way or another. Then for fear of being exposed by one of the "freshmen", we begin to cover ourselves in some way. When we discover that our cover does not change our inner self, we get caught in the undercurrent of looking for more effective "cover" techniques. We seldom notice that the one we are really trying to fool is ourselves.

The undercurrent of "I must" is the power of Sheol whether it be:

> Now I must know,
> I must know,
> Must know.

or:

> Now I must have,
> I must have,
> Must have.

or:

> Now I must be,
> I must be,
> Must be.

7

A BLOW TO THE HEAD

Dethroning the Intellect

The first year of my teaching at Eastern New Mexico University was another significant turning point in my life. Three distinctively different students contributed to the process of change. The battering ram which began to shake the security of my little academic castle was in the person of a young man named Joe. He was big and boisterous with a bellowing baritone voice, over six foot two, and almost two hundred pounds, full of anger and destruction. His favorite sport was boxing because it gave him a legitimate outlet for his hostility. He knew nothing of the meaning of fear, at least not as far as anyone could tell by watching him.

I am not sure why Joe enrolled in "Old Testament Survey" but there he was in my first lecture at Eastern. It did not take long to discover that he was as angry at God as he was at the world. In his tirades I could almost see the wrestling match between Jacob and the angel (Gen. 32:22-32) being re-enacted before my eyes. The big issue with Joe, as it related to the Old Testament, was the question of how a "good and loving God" could require so much blood-shed. He totally disrupted every lecture he attended with his railing accusations against God. Fortunately for the class, he was only present about one third of the time.

The questions he raised did not shake me, and I did not feel threatened by his size or his anger. I knew how to answer his questions from a biblical and theological point of view and was confident that my answers were valid. I could see that his concept of God (i.e., his God-image) was not accurate and that his notion of how things "ought" to be (i.e., his world-image) was unrealistic. I even had a measure of insight into the psychological dynamics which drove him to these denunciations of God. What bothered me was, first, that I could not get his attention long enough to give him my answers and, second, I knew that even if I could get his attention my answers would not help him with his struggle. His need was too deep to be touched by logical explanations.

I did not know how to respond to his constant barrage of blame and execration against God. Jesus had not defended Himself against the reviling of those who crucified Him. I knew that God was not the least bit threatened by this young man's upbraiding. God certainly did not need me to defend Him or to protect His name. He can take care of Himself. But Joe needed to experience the love and acceptance of God. There was no way he could receive that love as long as he continued to try to relate to God through his **false image of God.** As long as Joe thought of God as the angry vengeful disciplinarian, he would never be open to receive the love of God. There I was with no way to get his attention and with nothing to say but, "God loves you." For Joe's ears that sounded like a trite ecclesiastical slogan. Preachers are expected to say that.

After all those years of seeking and finding answers, my confidence in answers as such was now being shaken. During those difficult days I was asking myself whether the answers I had found would ever have any value beyond the classroom setting. I realized that I had been well equipped to help students fulfill their requirements for a degree, but I had nothing which could touch them in the place of their real need (at least not as far as I knew). I had knowledge from man, but the students needed life from God. This served to focus my attention on what had been happening to me over the years of preparation and training for ministry. I had been sidetracked.

The second thing that happened to prepare me for change was related to a student named Astrid. She was in my class on the "Book of Acts" and wanted to do her term paper on the phenomenon of speaking in tongues in the early church. Her choice of topics was not so unusual; many students are attracted to such topics because of a certain fascination for the mysterious. When she came in for her conference, however, I noticed a spark in her eyes which reminded me of the excitement I had known after the Lord had come to me in Japan. At the end of the semester she delivered her paper to me personally and gave testimony to some of the things God was doing in her life. I do not remember the details of what she shared, but I will never forget the sense of reality which prevailed as she spoke.

For the first time in several years I saw a ray of hope that I might be able to rekindle the flame which had been ignited in Japan, that I might again know the joy of walking daily with the Lord. Having lost confidence in the value of academic information apart from the real presence of God, I was ready for something. It had become obvious that the students needed—I needed—a personal living relationship with the living God. Mere information **about** God does not supply life to the inner man. With all my striving after answers, and finding some, I had come no closer to God. Ever-deepening insights into the doctrines of the Bible had failed to yield the quality of life I had known before; and I was hungry for that.

I began to seek after God with fresh expectation. I used what I honestly thought was the only faculty available to man by which he might seek after God: the mind. I was familiar with the idea that, within our inner being, "it is the Spirit himself bearing witness with our spirit that we are children of God" (Rom. 8:16). And I knew that "God is Spirit, and those who worship him must worship him in spirit and truth" (Jn. 4:24). But I did not understand that there is a clear and significant difference between the spirit and the mind of man. I had come to have an image of God as a glorified man with a glorified mind. I thought of an intellectual Bible scholar with strict self-discipline as a spiritual giant (provided, of course, that his doctrines were in agreement with the "truth" as "our group" taught it).

The second semester of my tenure at Eastern New Mexico University brought a third student into my life. Dick was a graduate student working toward his master's degree in religion. That term he was commuting from Lubbock, Texas, for the classes which met only once a week on Tuesdays. We quickly became friends during the morning and afternoon coffee breaks. Dick was the kind of person who liked to talk and who did not seem to notice whether the person he was talking to was listening or not. That bothered me until I started listening and discovered that he was not merely beating the breeze. He had something to say.

At first the topic of our discussions centered around some aspect of the class "Prophets of Israel." I had given a lecture on what I called "the prophetic experience", showing that the prophets were not speaking out of their heads but had experienced the real presence of the real God. In that lecture I had related the experience in Japan, suggesting that God still meets people in a real way today. In our conversation I sensed that he understood what I was talking about better than the other students did. In fact I began to suspect that he might even have a level of understanding beyond my own.

As our relationship developed other subjects often came up in our discussions. He had a unique ability to address himself to subjects which I was studying privately and to answer questions which were on my mind even though he had no way of knowing I was even thinking along those lines. In the beginning I attributed that to the fact that he just liked to talk and should be expected to ramble, at least occasionally, into a discussion of something I was wondering about. It soon became evident that it was not mere coincidence.

One day, for example, I was in my office studying Hebrews

4:12 where it speaks of the "division of soul and spirit" by the "living and active" word of God. My training had led me to believe that the soul and the spirit of man were essentially the same. I had also learned to equate the term "word of God" with the written text of the Bible. Now this written text was being referred to as living and active. I conjured up a vague image of the activity in man's mind when he read the text, and wondered if that was what this phrase "living and active" was intended to mean. But my real struggle was with this "division of soul and spirit." How could that which is essentially the same be divided? And what was the function of the written text in that process?

Dick knocked on the door, interrupting my thoughts, came in, seated himself and began to tell me some things he had read about the difference between soul and spirit. I listened with my feet propped up on my desk as he proceeded to answer, step by step, all the questions I was asking myself. During this one-sided conversation I never gave any indication that he was touching areas of serious questioning on my part. I wanted to see how far he would go without knowing what my inner response was. He just kept rambling (very systematically) until all the questions which were pressing me at that time had been satisfied.

Through his little "presentation" I saw that I had been approaching the issue of seeking after God with the wrong faculty. The mind of man is a function of his soul and is distinct from his spirit. There is a function called the mind of the spirit, but it does not receive its understanding from the efforts of man's logic. The mind of the spirit receives understanding through the **event** of God's revelation. When Peter recognized that Jesus was the Christ, the Son of the living God, Jesus told him, "...flesh and blood has not revealed this to you, but my Father who is in heaven" (Matt. 16:17). Peter had not gained that insight through his study of a written text, not even through his logical analysis of the events and teachings of Jesus. Many very bright and doctrinally informed Pharisees failed to receive that revelation because they approached Jesus through the faculty of their human logic. This revelation comes in the event of the "living and active word" doing its work in man's spirit. It is not a work of man, it is a work of God.

As Dick was drawing his comments to a close, my curiosity was aroused as never before. How was it possible for him to consistently answer questions, week after week, without even knowing I was asking? So I asked what had motivated him to come by the office at that particular time and talk about that particular topic. He said that the Spirit had prompted him to leave what he was doing and to come share those thought with me. I knew him to be an excellent student, and he was not a "flakey" person in any sense of the word, so I was not expecting an answer like that. I do not know if he noticed it or not, but I was in total shock when he left. I could not understand how a young man of his ability and perceptivity could make such a non-rational statement.

Being intellectually stimulated by the whole question of the Holy Spirit's involvement in daily life, I picked up some paper-back testimonials from the book store and began to read. Many interesting and exciting experiences were related in those books but, since I had no doctrinal cubby hole in which to place those phenomena, I was discounting most of what I read. I would not have called that unbelief. The church of my youth had never spoken of the Holy Spirit as a viable influence in a person's life beyond His function in the writing of the Bible. If anything like that had been taught in my college days I certainly had not had ears to hear. It was a completely new idea to me.

These three, Joe, Astrid and Dick, were instrumental in drawing my attention to the area of need. It was clear that man must seek after God by his spirit, not by his mind, because God is Spirit. And it was a relief to know that I would not have to understand God intellectually before He could move in my life again. But I was helpless to find a way out of the intellectual whirlpool in which I had been caught. I did not yet know how to exercise my spirit.

The more I read the more I desired the reality of it all but, at the same time, my well trained rational mind was discovering more convincing reasons why it was not really available. I was learning by experience that "the desires of the flesh are against the desires of the Spirit, and the desires of the Spirit are against the flesh" (Gal. 5:17). Every effort of the flesh (i.e., man's natural abilities apart from God) to draw near to God had placed a greater distance between myself and the realities I had known in Japan.

As it had been in Japan, this new turning did not take place as a result of any effort on my part. All my efforts were to no avail. The turning was an **event** which happened **to** me apart from any human act of readiness as such. In fact, like Saul of Tarsus (Acts 9:1-9), I was actually resisting it at the time. I was reading a book when it happened, but was in the process of explaining away each successive story as it was presented. The reservations I had concerning those testimonies were never consciously identified as unbelief any more than Saul would have recognized his zeal as being directed against the very God whom he thought he was serving. I considered it my responsibility before God to explain those stories to protect the young students on the campus from being carried away into false doctrines.

While I was reading, finding logical and doctrinal reasons for attributing every experience either to coincidence or to the over-active imagination of the author, suddenly, without warning, the Lord appeared in the room. It was not the sweet presence of "liquid love" as it had been in Japan. This time He appeared as "LORD" in the full meaning of the term. His presence evoked a sense of holy fear rather than tender devotion. It was a kind of fear I had never known before. His presence was not frightening, it was kingly, overpowering, awesome. I "saw" Him out of the corner of my eye, so to speak, though it was not a seeing of the eye. I think I could have counted the locks of His hair if I had looked squarely at Him. But I dared not look. His presence was too awe-full.

Not knowing what else to do, I asked, "Is that you, Lord?" I do not know why I asked that question, because there was no doubt in my mind who it was. The moment I asked, He spoke to me deep in my spirit. It was not a speaking to the consciousness, so I did not know what He had said, but I knew that He had spoken (Later, I also knew what He had said).I began to cry and sob. The words, "I'm sorry, I'm sorry," kept coming out of my mouth from somewhere deep within. I did not know what the apologizing was all about except that it had something to do with what He had said. The weeping continued for about half an hour. Afterward I felt very clean, and there was a new freshness inside. Whatever had happened was real and effective. Whatever He had said had come as a "living and active word" which accomplished its intended work within me even without my conscious understanding.

There was a new zest for life after this, just as there had been when He came with His loving acceptance while I was in the Air Force. Things began to change so rapidly from that time forward that it would be difficult for me to piece together a chronological sequence of how it all came about. I did not understand what had happened or what it was all supposed to mean. He had not come to give understanding, He had come to bring me out of death into life. One thing I did understand, however, was that He who had come to me with love and acceptance before had now shown Himself as the one having all authority in heaven and on earth. In Japan He had revealed His unconditional love. In New Mexico He revealed His unconditional Lordship.

During the next few months I read everything I could get my hands on that dealt with the Holy Spirit as a present and active reality in the lives of Christians. My eyes had somehow been opened to see things in a new light. It was clear to me now that it was the Holy Spirit who had made the presence of the Lord so real to me in Japan. The problem was that I had not yet learned to relate that experience to my life as a whole. I had seen no need to integrate it into my theology. It was something which had happened "once upon a time, in a land far away." I had come to think of it as subject matter for academic investigation rather than as something to provide a dynamic for daily living. It had come to be very little more than an illustration to add a personal touch to my teaching.

That was all beginning to change now, and I was excited again. The first obvious change was in the area of Bible reading. After visiting with Dick until about eleven p.m. one evening, I decided to read a while before going to bed. I opened the Bible to the book of Romans and began to read. The book came alive to me. It was as though I had never read it before in my whole life. I had taken "Romans" in undergraduate school and had translated the entire book from the Greek as a graduate student. I had even taught through the book several times on the college level. I thought I knew what was in there, and I did as far as its logical and doctrinal context was concerned.

This time it was different. I was being fed in my spirit. I was receiving life from every page. It was an exciting book. After completing Romans, I moved on to the Corinthian letters, then to Galatians and Ephesians. Every word was alive and breathing. I continued to read until I had finished all of Paul's letters. At three a.m. I finally put the Bible down, having read things I had never noticed before and having received a "living word" from verses which previously had been mere statements of doctrine. It was obvious something very real had happened. I came to realize later that a division of soul and spirit had taken place within me as I was receiving the work of the living and active word of God.

Without being aware of it I had picked up a spirit of intellectualism in the process of striving for an education. In using knowledge as a cover-up for a poor self-image I had exalted the mind to the throne of my life and it had begun to usurp the authority and function of the Holy Spirit, as though the natural mind could lead a man in the ways of God or to the truth of God (cf. Jn. 16:13). I had made a covenant with intellectualism. My "friend" protected me from being exposed as a dumb-dumb in exchange for the right to censure everything that filtered through my *psyche* (from the Greek, meaning soul or mind). This "friend" would not allow anything to come from my inner spirit into consciousness without some re-definition or logical qualification. It was this intellectual spirit which had been explaining away everything I read.

I had learned to depend upon the human psyche governed by the spirit of intellectualism for guidance and for understanding

Scripture. The spirit in me which had been born of the "living and abiding word of God" (I Pet. 1:23), and which had been quickened in Japan, was suffering from malnutrition. My natural mind was not allowing any "word-food" to pass through the circuits of the logical censuring process. Because of this, all my attempts to break through to God had ended in failure. But now God had broken through to me. He triumphed over my intellectualism and established Himself as Lord over my heart.

That night, when I was reading Paul's letters and receiving so much life, it was not my effort that brought the Scriptures to life. That experience had been preceded by many years of study, proving my inability to find God through my own intellectual efforts. All my efforts to discover God in the Sciptures had been unfruitful. But now God was "discovering" Himself to me by His Spirit. I know from experience that the "written code kills, but the spirit gives life" (II Cor. 3:6). With "unveiled face" I had beheld the "glory of the Lord" while reading Scipture (II Cor. 3:18). Over a period of time I began to have more confidence in the unsolicited insights which came during my private Bible study time. When I saw that the sharing of those insights brought life to the students I knew there was reality in what I was seeing. It was not long before I even had an opportunity to pray for Joe (who had given me so much trouble in "Old Testament Survey"). It was a touching sight to behold that hulk of a man on his knees in humility asking Jesus to be Lord of his life.

As the process of dethroning the intellect continued, various thoughts and insights continued to "gurgle up" from deep within, that is, from the same source from which the crying and sobbing had come when His lordship was revealed. These thoughts did not originate with my intellect, nor could the insights be attributed to my human ability to discover truth. As I became more sensitive to those musings of the mind of the spiritual man, I could even hear the words which He had spoken to me at the revelation of His Lordship. They were still "echoing" in my spirit. He had said, "Fount, you have not been believing me, have you?" The tone of His voice was still very real even though it had been several months since He had confronted me. There was no condemnation in His voice toward me, only a loving concern that I walk under His Lordship. It is no wonder I had begun to sob, saying, "I'm sorry, I'm sorry." I had been offending His love and rejecting the impulses of His Spirit.

Since that time there has never been any serious doubt in my mind that there is a clear distinction between the soul and the spirit of man. After years of trying to find God with my mind, my spirit had heard the voice of the Lord and had responded in repentance while my conscious mind was unaware of what had been said. My spirit had cried while my soul was wondering what was happening. I knew I was not having a "break-down" because I was at peace within myself at the time. I was fully aware of my conscious thoughts, knowing that the Lord was doing a deep work but having no idea of what that work was all about.

His words had been spoken clearly and effectively to my spirit but had not been admitted into the conscious mind until the intellectual spirit had been effectively driven from the throne. The fact that those words were still almost audibly present in my spirit (ready to be "heard" by the conscious mind as soon as it had come under submission to the spirit), was to me a sign of the reality of the spiritual nature as distinct from the soulish nature of the man who has been born again. I came to realize that one can have the Spirit as his **life source** without necessarily allowing the Spirit to effect his **life style** (Gal. 5:25). One can be born of the Spirit without walking by the Spirit. Much of my preparation for the teaching ministry had been little more than an attempt to gratify the desires of my "flesh" in its striving for a place of honor in this world.

It is true that the two words, soul (*psyche*) and spirit (*pneuma*), are often used interchangeably in the Bible to refer to the inner man as distinct from the outward man. When a clear distinction is needed, however, the New Testament writers often use another term "flesh" (*sarx*), to refer to man's soulish nature in its opposition to the Spirit of God. In this context, "flesh" does not refer to the "meaty" portions of the physical body. The "desires of the flesh" mentioned above are not limited to the impulses and cravings of the natural body. The "works of the flesh" include such things as "enmity, strife, jealousy, anger, selfishness, dissension, party spirit" (Gal. 5:20) and many other expressions of the soul in its self-exaltation and self-assertion. It was the desire of my flesh to cover up the dumb-dumb self-image. It was the desire of my flesh to impress people with my knowledge of scripture. It was the desire of my flesh to have others think of me as a spiritual giant.

With this insight, I realized what Paul meant when he asked, "Are you so foolish? Having begun with the Spirit, are you now ending with the flesh?" (Gal. 3:4). My walk with the Lord had been initiated by the Spirit in Japan, but I had been trying to bring myself to maturity in Christ by my own natural abilities. I had tried to learn how to proclaim the testimony of God in lofty words of man's wisdom and, because of that, there had been no "demonstration of the Spirit and of power" (I Cor. 2:1-5). Having placed my faith in human wisdom, no power of life was made available through my teaching.

What we often fail to take into account in our seeking after God is the fact that Adam died, and he remains dead to the things of God. We have defined death as the falling out of correspondence with environment, i.e., being separated from the relationships necessary for the sustenance of life. The adamic nature, which we have received through our natural birth, is separated from the source of divine life. He whose seed was responsible for our human nature was separated from the tree of life when he ate from the tree of the knowledge of good and evil. Adam's nature is still very much alive in its ability to exercise its earthly appetites and to express its hostility to the things of the spirit, but it can only produce death as far as any relationship with God is concerned (see Fig. #4).

On the other hand, Jesus Christ "being raised from the dead will never die again; death no longer has dominion over him. The death he died he died to sin, once for all, but the life he lives he lives to God" (Rom. 6:9,10). As Adam's death was unto God and his life unto sin, so Christ's death was unto sin and his life unto God. As we participate in Adam's death unto God by virtue of our natural birth, so we participate in Christ's life unto God

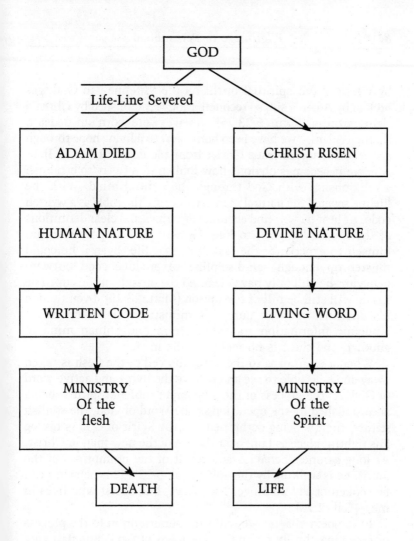

FIGURE #4

TWO DESTINIES

by virtue of our spiritual birth. As the "lifeline" to God was broken by Adam's sin, so reconciliation is established by Christ's righteousness (Rom. 5:23,25). As we were born unto death through Adam, "we have been born anew to a living hope through the resurrection of Jesus Christ from the dead" (I Pet. 1:3).

Here it becomes obvious how foolish it is to try to establish a relationship with God through the natural mind. With the lifeline severed the natural man can only see the Bible as a written code. At best he will find accurate doctrines and clear definitions of the life he "ought" to live. He will find no power within himself to experience the reality of that life. Even if he could muster up enough self-discipline to produce good outward behavior, he will only have cleansed the outside of the cup. The inside will still be full of corruption (Matt. 23:25). Even though his doctrines may be pure, his ministry will be limited to academic information transferred from one human mind to another; and there is no reality of life in that.

When a man turns to the Lord, the veil of the flesh is taken away and he is able to see and receive the living and active word of God. As the process of the division of soul and spirit is being accomplished by the operation of the Word of God, the soulish natural man is being dethroned and the Spirit of God is taking His rightful place as Lord over the life of the new man in Christ. As long as one's behavior is a result of the promptings of the Spirit, he is walking by the Spirit (Gal. 5:25). This behavior can be spoken of as "no longer I who live, but Christ who lives in me" (Gal. 2:20).

In the next chapter we will turn our attention to the process of receiving the living and active word of God. But first, my reader, if you have not yet received the word of God as seed, open your heart to Him now and He will meet you as you pray. Simply turn your back on the old Adam nature and its history of resistance and turn your face toward God. Ask Him to manifest His love to you in the forgiveness of your sin. The promise is yours: "...if you confess with your lips that Jesus is Lord and believe in your heart that God raised him from the dead, you will be saved. For man believes with his heart and so is justified, and he confesses with his lips and so is saved. The scripture says, "No one who believes in him will be put to shame." (Rom. 10:9-12).

8

THE IMPLANTED WORD

God's Provision for Wholeness

We have noticed that seed reproduces after its kind. The nature of the offspring is determined by the **seed** of its generation. We inherited our human nature from Adam through the meditation of our earthly parentage. We have also noticed that our self-image develops through receiving a **formative word** from the important others during childhood. That word (in my case "dumb-dumb") also has an effect on the development of certain behavior patterns which we divided into two categories: 1) cover-up and 2) exposure. In the first case, one is trying to hide his true nature (as he conceives it) lest he be rejected. In the second, one is exposing his true nature in an attempt to find someone who will love him for what he is. Finally we saw that when one is born of the "living and abiding word of God" he receives a seed from above which creates in him a new nature with the capacity of being conformed to the image of God's Son (Rom. 8:29).

In this chapter we will begin to turn our attention to the process of receiving the new image, becoming "partakers of the divine nature" (II Pet. 1:4) which is "created after the likeness of

God in true righteousness and holiness" (Eph. 4:24). To aid the reader in following this presentation we have structured the discussion under four headings: 1) the **principle,** 2) the **problem,** 3) the **promise** and 4) the **program.** After these we will close this chapter with a discussion of God's offer to those who will take the position of humility.

As the self-image of the old man developed through receiving a formative word so the image of the new man will develop as he receives from his new Father "the implanted word which is able to save your soul" (Jas. 1:21). The basic principle of spiritual development is stated in this verse but some explanation is necessary to see the significance of it.

The eternal **Word,** who was in the beginning with God and who was Himself God, became flesh in the person of Jesus Christ (Jn. 1:1,14). Within His "loins" was the word-seed which is now available to man through the death, burial and resurrection. When we receive that word-seed through reading or hearing the Word proclaimed it begins to grow and develop within. Although we may be immediately conscious of certain external changes, it takes time to become conscious of the full reality of the new creation (II Cor. 5:17). As we slowly became aware of ourselves in our natural environment as growing human beings, so we must also grow in our awareness of the spiritual "self" in its divine environment. This is what it means to increase in the knowledge of God (Col. 1:10).

As the new nature becomes aware of itself in its spiritual environment, it can begin to receive the word of its Father. The Word of God then becomes a formative element in the growth and development of the new born child of God. This is what Peter meant when he wrote, "like new born babes, long for the pure spiritual milk, that by it you may grow up to salvation" (I Pet. 2:2). Peter's phrase, "spiritual milk", could be translated literally as "word-milk." To grasp the significance of this phrase, let us make a comparison. If we have a baby produced by dog-seed we call it a baby dog, and we are not surprised to discover that it is hungry for dog-milk. A baby produced by word-seed might be called a baby word and should be expected to be hungry for word-milk. So we understand word-milk here as a formative element in the development of the new nature.

In our natural development there is always a measure of contradiction between what we are by **nature** and the **word** which we receive from our natural parentage. Sometimes our problems as human beings derive from the fact that we are trying to live up to a self-image received from a word which is more than, or different from, what our natural abilities can handle. At other times we have conflicts because we are trying to live down a self-image received from a word which is below our capacity. In either case, the struggle comes from the **inconsistency** between what we **received from the SEED** and what we **received from the WORD** of our parentage. To facilitate our discussion here, we will present another diagram (see Fig. #5).

In this diagram we have indicated that there is no inconsistency between the **nature** we receive as children of God and the **image** we receive from the Word which tells us who we are in Christ. The same Word (which is God Himself) is both seed and nourishment for the new man. The Word which our heavenly Father speaks to us as His sons is consistent with the Word of our regeneration. And, since this Word generates within us the divine nature, there is nothing in our new image to cause shame. There is nothing to cover up, no cause for any fear of being exposed. When the new man behaves according to his nature that which comes forth is an expression of the nature of God the Word. The behavior of the old man is at best a religious or social cover-up (which is hypocrisy and therefore really worse).

The **problem** is that both the old and the new abide in the same body. The fleshly nature and the spiritual nature of man "are opposed to each other, to prevent you from doing what you would" (Gal. 5:17). It is possible for both blessings and curses to come from the same mouth because there are two "springs" inside, one pouring forth "fresh water" and the other "brackish" (Jas. 3:10,11). So there is a war in our members, and the objective of the new man in Christ is to "put off" the old nature with its corrupt behavior patterns and to "put on the new nature, created after the likeness of God in true righteousness and holiness" (Eph.

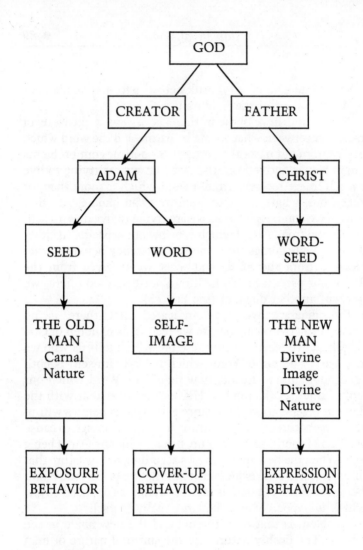

FIGURE #5

MAN INTEGRATED IN CHRIST

4:22-24). Keeping with our analogy of articles of clothing this would be expressed as taking off the armors, the overcoats, the three-piece suits and even the T-shirts of our old self-image. And it means accepting and putting on the reality of who we are in Christ Jesus.

The problem is further complicated, however, by the fact that the old nature is already well established in its image and behavior before the new nature comes to consciousness. When the new born babe in Christ becomes aware of his new nature then the old nature, being established as lord over this life, often tries to produce the "true righteousness and holiness" by the strength and wisdom of his humanity. The righteousness produced in this way can never be more than a cover for iniquity. "We have all become like one who is unclean, and all our righteous deeds are like a polluted garment" (Isa. 64:6). So we must also take off our religious garments. When we try to reflect the image of God as a work of the flesh it is a distorted image and is considered idolatry and sorcery (Gal. 5:20).

Only the true God can produce true righteousness and holiness. That which is flesh is flesh and can only produce a religious pretense. Man as man can only produce a vain image of God from the vain imagination of man. Any time man exalts himself or any product of his humanity to the position of deity he exchanges the "truth about God for a lie" and worships "the creature rather than the creator" (Rom. 1:25). "Can a man make for himself gods? Such are no gods!" (Jer. 16:20). Any holiness which we produce of ourselves and present to others as true holiness is a holiness produced by a god which is no god. As man cannot create a god which is real neither can he produce a godliness which is true to God's holiness.

But, on the other hand, the **promise** is that God has given us the right to become children of God through Jesus Christ (Jn. 1:13). Those who are born of God are predestined to be conformed to the image of His first-born Son (Rom. 8:29). We have the potential of sharing His glory (Rom. 8:17) and of participating in His divine nature (II Pet. 1:4). This is no vain expectation of some ego maniac; it is the promise of God offered to those who will walk in the way of His leading. Those who are led by the Spirit are sons of God (Rom. 8:14). Nor is this conformity to His image something which we can comprehend now. "It does not yet appear what we shall be. But we know that when he appears **we shall be like him,** for we shall see him as he is (I Jn. 3:2, emphasis mine). Our expectation should be that we will enter into the reality of that not only in some sort of inner feeling but in our **conduct.**

There is only one way that we can ever really expect such a miracle. When it is "no longer I who live, but Christ who lives in me" (Gal. 2:20), the "Christ in me" can and will live a life of true righteousness and holiness. He is the only one who can live that kind of life. That life is not a **pretense,** it is the **presence** of the Father abiding in the new man (Jn. 14:20-24). What God demands and expects of us is **His own holiness.** "As he who called you is holy, be holy yourselves in all your conduct" (I Pet. 1:15). This holiness of both person and conduct can only be accomplished by "Christ in you, the hope of glory" (Col. 1:27).

As we noticed above, the problem is that both "selves" live in the same body. This difficulty is insurmountable apart from the continuing work of God. He can overcome every obstacle and He will in those who are willing to lay down the "self-life" and follow the leading of His Spirit. This is the negative work that needs to be done. It is only "by the Spirit" that we are able to "put to death the deeds of the body" (Rom. 8:13). We must be willing to deny ourselves and take up our cross daily, for "whoever would save his life (i.e., self-life) will lose it; and whoever loses his life for my sake, will save it" (Lk. 9:23,24). If we desire to be resurrected to a new life we must be willing to die to the old. The old must die before the new can live. And both must be a work of the Spirit; neither can be accomplished by the flesh.

It is encouraging to know that, "though our outer nature (the old man) is wasting away, our inner nature (the new man) is being renewed every day" (II Cor. 4:16). Even though the old nature had a head start, it is fighting a losing battle in those who are willing to die to themselves and come alive unto God as Jesus

Christ did in His humanity.

So we see that it is the Father's intention to bring believers to the point of being conformed to the image of His Son. When Scripture speaks of bringing "many sons to glory" (Heb. 2:10) it speaks of God's intention concerning those who are born of the living Word. His desire is to bring those born into His family to a level of maturity in which they are able to reflect the glory of God in their character and conduct. As a metter of fact, **the basic desire of fatherhood** as such is to see **His own image and likeness reproduced** in His sons. It is also true that **the reality of sonship** as such is seen in **the capacity to grow into the likeness of the Father.** So this image and likeness of God the Father is the ultimate destiny of those who participate in divine sonship.

Biblically speaking, then, there is much more involved in "salvation" than a promise of heaven after we die. Eternal life is more than the continuation of existence over an infinitely long period of time. It is a quality of life which is available only in Christ Jesus. Any teaching which offers "heaven some day" with no power to live a life of godliness here and now is only a partial gospel. "He who believes in the Son has eternal life" (Jn. 3:36). The Word "has" indicates a present reality, not merely a future promise. The eternal life which Jesus offers is the abundant life (Jn. 10:10) which Ruth Paxon called "life on the highest plane." It is life in Christ here and now; it will continue in eternity, but it has its beginnings and reality here and now (all this and heaven too!).

The issue of God's **program** for our wholeness comes into focus as we read "...receive with **meekness** the **implanted** word which is able to **save your souls**" (Jas. 1:21, emphasis mine). James identifies his readers as those who, by the will of God, have been brought forth by the word of truth (Jas. 1:18). That is to say, the ones to whom he addresses his remarks have been born of the Word. The popular concept of salvation is brought into question when we see the implications of this verse. James is suggesting that those to whom he is writing (i.e., born again believers) **still have need of salvation in their souls.** This seems to indicate that being born of the Spirit is not strictly equal to the salvation of the soul. Here it becomes evident that the experience of being born again is the **beginning** but the salvation of the soul is a **continuing program** of God for those who are born into His family.

A closer look at Peter's writings gives the same impression. Having stated that "we have been born anew," he allows that we "may have to suffer various trials" so that our faith may be tested as by fire. The goal of these trials is seen in the fact that "as the outcome of your faith you obtain the **salvation of your souls**" (I Pet. 1:3-9, emphasis mine). It seems clear enough that it is the ones who are born anew whose faith might be tried. It seems equally evident that the outcome of that trial, which is subsequent to being born anew, is the salvation of their souls. Both James and Peter have thus spoken of salvation as a process which continues after one has been born into the family of God. So the new birth might be compared to the draft while the salvation of the soul is like a boot camp training program.

This highlights our need for a more complete definition and understanding of the word "salvation." Since both Peter and James have also referred to the "soul" as the object of that continuing salvation, we will briefly consider the nature and function of the soul as it relates to life and conduct.

The basic idea of the word translated "to save" can be illustrated most clearly in the context of physical healing. When Jairus came to Jesus his daughter was at the point of death. He besought Jesus to come and lay His hands on her that she might be made well (Mk. 5:23). The word translated "made well" is a form of the same word which James and Peter use for salvation. That word also appears later when a woman with an issue of blood touched the hem of His garment and was made well (v. 34).

The word is often translated "to rescue" or "to deliver." More than that, however, it pictures a state of well being in which the one who has been delivered is not only free from the difficulty or danger which was threatening but also safe from any continuing harm or lingering after effects. We see here both a positive and a negative aspect of healing (or salvation). The daughter of Jairus was not only rescued from the negative work of death, she was also brought into a state of positive health and well being. The body of the woman was delivered from the ailment and given health and wholeness. Because of the healing (saving) work of Jesus both of these physical bodies were able to function properly (the positive aspect) having been delivered from death and sickness (the negative aspect).

With this understanding of salvation (healing) the statements of James and Peter begin to make more sense. **As the new born babe begins to receive the implanted word** (Jas. 1:21) **or the word-milk** (I Pet. 2:2), **the soul experiences deliverance from bondages** (the negative "putting off") **and is brought into an ever improving condition of health and wholeness** (the positive "putting on"). As the body is able to function properly after a sickness to the degree that it experiences complete healing, so the soul can begin to function under the leadership of the Spirit to the degree that it experiences the continuing salvation process.

What, then, is ill health in relation to the soul? Or, to ask the same question in a different way, what does "wholeness' mean as far as the soul is concerned? First we must notice that the **soul is the behavior mechanism of man,** i.e., it is the man himself with his various appetites, thought patterns and emotional responses which cause him to behave the way he does. With this understanding the concept of the salvation of the soul becomes clear. The "saved soul" is one which has been delivered out of the bondages of its unhealthy appetites, deceptive thought patterns and improper emotional responses (the negative) and has been brought into a state of wholeness in which it can function under God (the positive). Being free from the hindrances and contrary impulses of the "old man" he is now free to respond to the impulses of the Holy Spirit.

We have noticed that the word translated "soul" is *psyche*. This word comes into the English language in the formation of words such as "psychology." A psychologist is one who studies the behavior patterns and responses of men and animals. The appearance of the word "behavior" here draws attention to the reason for our interest in the psyche. As the behavior mechanism, the soul is responsible for the processing of information and the making of decisions concerning what to do. It is the psyche which "translates" our thoughts and feelings (both conscious and unconscious) into action. It is the psyche which responds to a threat or to an offer of love. It is responsible for the **cover-up** and the **exposure** as well as for the **expression** of God's nature which comes through obedience to the impulses of the Spirit of God.

This is where the healing (salvation) of the soul comes in. Our purpose as sons of God is to put off the old nature which is corrupt through deceitful lusts (Eph. 4:22). This is the negative aspect of the salvation of the soul. That is to say, we must be set free from the bondages within the psyche before we can hope to mature in Christ. We must be liberated from the forces which drive us to continue the pretense of cover-up, from the continual inner striving for that which is empty and fruitless. And we must be delivered from the impulses which move us to expose the evil nature of the old man with his self-image.

But we are also called to "put on then, as God's chosen ones, holy and beloved, compassion, kindness, lowliness, meekness, and patience" (Col. 3:12). These are not merely inner feelings or attitudes; they are "put on" only to the degree that they show forth in our conduct with our fellow man. Nor can these qualities be produced by the natural man (except as counterfeit, which is like a polluted garment). The putting on of these virtues requires the positive aspect of the salvation of the soul. The process of salvation brings the psyche into a state of positive wholeness in which it can be responsive to the Holy Spirit.

With this understanding of salvation (as both healing and wholeness), a person can be placed into one of **three basic categories:** 1) soulish, 2) fleshly, or 3) spiritual. These three categories are presented in I Cor. 2:14-3:3 to which we will turn shortly. Each of these categories can be viewed from either of **two perspectives:** 1) position or 2) walk (see Fig. #6). There are only **two positions.** A man is either in Christ or he is in Adam (I Cor. 15:22, Rom. 5:12-21). And there are only **two sources of behavior.** A man is either walking according to the flesh or he is walking according to the Spirit (Gal. 5:16-26; Rom. 8:5-8).

The soulish man (i.e., the one whose basic source of life is

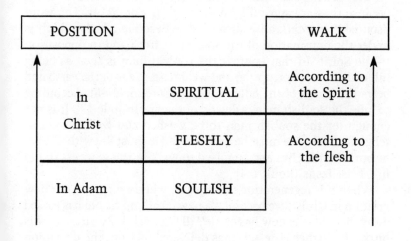

FIGURE #6

POSITION AND WALK

his own psyche) "does not receive the gifts of the Spirit of God, for they are folly to him, and he is not able to understand them because they are spiritually discerned" (I Cor. 2:14). The word "soulish" (*psychikon*) is also used to describe a body which is under the domination of the soul apart from and in opposition to the Spirit. In that context the soulish man is seen as being full of dishonor, corruption and weakness. He is of the earth and bears the image of the fallen Adam (I Cor. 15:42-48). According to Jude the soulish man is devoid of the Spirit (Jude 19). It is not enough for the soulish man to be washed and well dressed in religious deeds. He must be born anew. He must die with Christ, be buried with Him and be raised to walk in the newness of life in Christ Jesus (Rom. 6:4).

When this regeneration takes place, when we receive our new position in Christ, we become "a new creation; the old has passed away, behold, the new has come" (II Cor. 5:17). By virtue of this birth, the Father Himself "has delivered us from the dominion of darkness and transferred us to the kingdom of his beloved Son" (Col. 3:13), and we stand before Him justified rather than condemned (Rom. 3:23,24). We who were enemies in Adam have now been reconciled to God in Christ (II Cor. 5:18). All this is accomplished by the grace of God apart from any human work. It is a gift of God (Eph. 2:8,9).

The arrow at the left of the diagram (Fig. #6) indicates this change which takes place as an event, once for all. Our **position** is altered radically when we are born into God's family. We are no longer in Adam, we are in Christ. By virtue of our being "in Christ" we are in a position of victory over the bondages of the soul because He has broken their power through His death and resurrection. This position is a reality which is ours **in Christ** even though we may not yet have realized it in our daily experience; "we are more than conquerors through him who loved us" (Rom. 8:37). "He disarmed the principalities and powers and made a public example of them, triumphing over them in him" (Col. 2:15), and we are in Him! We are seated "with him in the heavenly places in Christ Jesus" (Eph. 2:6). **This is the position we have in Christ Jesus!**

But we must understand that the Father has changed our position in order that He might begin to change our walk. "For we are his workmanship (like a craft project), created in Christ Jesus **for good works**..." (Eph. 2:10, emphasis mine). We who are "in Christ" have that position by virtue of the creative work of the Father. He brought us into a covenant relationship with Himself by His work of grace. Man does not come into this relationship with God by the strength of human effort. But God did not create this "new man" merely to be there or bring him into relationship with Himself simply to exist in Christ. He created him to be involved in the good works "which God prepared beforehand that we should walk in them" (Eph. 2:10). But by the same token these works which are prepared for us are not deeds which we are able to accomplish apart from the continuing work of God in our behalf. They are rather the outworking of the relationship we have with God through the Christ who is working in us.

Now there are also two categories among those whose position has been altered: 1) the fleshly man who is a babe in Christ (I Cor. 3:1) and 2) the spiritual man who "judges all things, but is himself judged (understood) by no one" (I Cor. 2:15). Paul said of the first group that their fleshly nature was demonstrated by the fact that envy, strife and division were manifest among them. Envy and strife come either from the exercise of self-will and self-exaltation or from feelings of being slighted and deprived of ones rights. Self-will and self-exaltation are infirmities within the soul of the fleshly christian and they hinder him from a life of walking by the Spirit. He has not yet put off the old man; he has not died to himself. His soul is in need of healing (salvation) in that respect.

Paul asked the fleshly babes in Christ, "Are you not of the flesh, and **behaving like ordinary men?**" (I Cor. 3:3, emphasis mine). It is the mark of the fleshly christian that an outsider cannot tell by his behavior that he is in Christ. The babe in Christ, as far as his **position** is concerned, but he does not **walk** (or behave) like Christ. We have seen that behavior is processed through the soul in accord with its appetites, thoughts and emotional condition. Coming to maturity in Christ as spiritual men is therefore a life-long **process** of receiving with meekness the implanted Word and allowing that living and active Word to have its effect of salvation within the soul. The arrow at the right of our chart (Fig. #6) indicates a continued process rather than a one time experience.

The spiritual man is one whose soul has been healed to the point of being able to produce the true righteousness and holiness of which we have spoken. This is the goal which Paul had in mind when he said, "Brethren, I do not consider that I have made it my own; but one thing I do, forgetting what lies behind and straining forward to what lies ahead, I press on toward the goal for the prize of the upward call of God in Christ Jesus" (Phil. 3:13,14). If we see this maturity level as a **state of sanctification** into which we should enter immediately, our life will either be filled with frustration in trying to accomplish that sanctification or with pretense and cover-up in trying to convince ourselves and others that we have arrived. But when we recognize it as a **process of becoming in our walk** what we **already are in our position**, each new day provides a new excitement in the possibility of "being changed into his likeness from one degree of glory to another" (II Cor. 3:18).

How then do we move toward the goal? How do we "receive with meekness the implanted word" which will bring our soul toward this new level of wholeness? I can certainly testify that it is not enough to apply ones natural mind to the scriptures with human diligence. Studying the Bible and memorizing favorite passages will not, in itself, accomplish the desired goal. Maturity of the spiritual man does not come by soulish effort. Like the initial justification, it is "not because of deeds done by us in righteousness" (Tit. 3:5). We must continually remember Paul's question, "Are you so foolish? Having begun with the Spirit, are you now ending (i.e., coming to maturity) with the flesh?" (Gal. 3:3). Since we came to our new position by the operation of the Spirit, we must also come to maturity by the Spirit (Gal. 5:25).

The putting off of the old nature must not—indeed it cannot—be the work of the arm of flesh. "But if by the Spirit you put to death the deeds of the body you will live" (Rom. 8:13). The soul cannot redeem itself, neither can it heal itself of its mortal disease. It must depend upon the work of the Spirit. Nor can the soul do the positive work of changing itself into a state of wholeness. It cannot put on the new nature by a work of obedience motivated or accomplished in the strength of Adam. That would again be the polluted garment of human righteousness. As we received Christ by receiving the Word of justification, so we mature in Christ by receiving the Word of salvation (healing) in faith. As babes in Christ we must long for the word-milk by which growth unto salvation comes.

If study and memorization of the Bible will not, in itself, produce the desired end then how do we go about receiving the Word? The process of getting ourselves in a position to receive the reality of the living and active Word is the theme of the next chapter. Here we will look at the offer which God makes to those who will take the position of humility trusting Him to do the work.

There is hope offered in II Cor. 3:18, but there is a necessary prerequisite to receiving the offer. Several comments will be helpful in preparation to really "hear" the offer. First, the general context of the chapter is contrasting the elements of the new covenant to the elements of the old covenant. In the chart (see Fig. #7) we notice that there are "writings" in both covenants, but the writing of the old is with ink while the writing of the new is by the Spirit. The first is written upon stone tablets while the second is written upon human hearts. And there are "ministries" in both covenants. The ministry of the old brings death but the ministry of the new brings life. The first comes with a passing glory which fades away; the second comes with surpassing glory which endures. For one there is a veil and for the other the veil is removed. This removing of the veil is the necessary prerequisite to receiving the promise offered.

The second thing which requires comment is the way in which Paul uses the concept of "veil" to make his point. Moses is presented as putting the veil over his face "so that the Israelites might not see the end (i.e., the full extent) of the fading splendor"

OLD	NEW
WRITTEN WITH INK	WRITTEN BY THE SPIRIT
ON STONE TABLETS	ON THE HEART
MINISTRY OF DEATH	MINISTRY OF LIFE
PASSING GLORY FADES	SURPASSING GLORY
VEIL SEPARATES	VEIL IS REMOVED

FIGURE #7

LIFE AND DEATH

(II Cor. 3:13). The interpretation of the word "end" to mean "full extent" seems necessary for two reasons. In the first place the original story (Ex. 34) gives no indication that Moses was afraid that the people might notice that the glow was diminishing. On the contrary, he put the veil on because the people were intimidated by the shining glory even though it was fading. In the second place, following the mention of the veil, Paul said that the people's minds were hardened. His point is that the people were unwilling to look upon the reflected glory of God in the face of Moses in spite of the fact that it was only a fading splendor. The hardness of the people's heart was responsible for the veil because they did not want to look at the full extent of the glory reflected on Moses' face.

This veil, then, becomes a symbol of the hardness of heart which refuses to look upon the reflected glory of the Lord. In Exodus 19 and 20 this hardness of heart is seen when the people refuse to hear the voice of God Himself and insist that Moses go hear from God for them. Since God had said, "...if you will obey (hear) my voice..." (Ex. 19:5), it appears that their refusal to hear (Ex. 20:18) may have been responsible for the written code in the first place. The natural man is always threatened when face to face with the real glory of the real God even if it is only in a reflected form as it was on Moses' face. The light of God's presence exposes the flesh for what it is, and those who do not want to have their deeds exposed as evil, always flee from the light (Jn. 3:18). Only those who are willing to admit that they do not already have what they need are in a position to rejoice when the light comes. They know they need light.

It is easy enough for the flesh to look at a scroll. Even if it is a "holy" scroll one can read it and find a way to excuse or cover himself. Or one might even be able to convince himself that he is abiding by the principles contained in the written code, at least as long as he is only challenged by other men who are no better than he is. After all, is it not the man himself who interprets the scroll for himself? But when one is face to face with the glory of God (even in its reflected form) he is exposed, undone and without excuse. It is no wonder religious men prefer a written code to the presence of God. But the offer of this passage is not for those who would arrogantly hold to their understanding of a written text. It is for the poor in spirit.

Next Paul makes a shift in his use of the concept of the veil. He transferred it from Moses' face to the heart, or mind, of the one who reads the written code. "Yes, to this day, whenever Moses is read, a veil lies over their minds" (II Cor. 3:15). The third issue which requires comment, then, is Paul's references to the reading of Moses and the old covenant. The phrase "old covenant" might lead some to think that Paul was talking about reading the books of the Hebrew Bible since this phrase is sometimes rendered "Old Testament." Nothing could be farther from his intention.

The New Testament as we know it had not yet been written. What we call the Old Testament was the only Holy Scripture available to the early church. By means of those writings the early evangelists were able to confute the unbelieving Jews "showing by the scriptures that Christ was Jesus" (Acts 18:28). Jesus Himself said, "You search the scriptures, for in them you think you have eternal life; and it is they that bear witness to me" (Jn. 5:39).

How could Paul suggest that the scriptures which bear witness to Jesus Christ have a ministry of death? But those to whom Jesus spoke were unable to see that testimony because of the veil on their hearts and minds. The difficulty was not with the text as such but with the hardness of the human heart which refuses to open itself up to the light of His glory. "How can you believe, who receive glory from one another and do not seek the glory that comes from the only God?" (Jn. 5:44).

As we follow Paul's line of reasoning, we see that he was suggesting that many in his day were reading the scriptures in such a way as to be totally unaware of the glory of the Lord which was reflected there. When we apply this insight to our generation, we must be alerted to the fact that it is also possible for us to read the New Testament with a veil over our minds. We can read the text of the New Testament as a written code just as surely as they did the Old Testament. Some read and see only doctrines, others read and see only rules and regulations concerning an external form of godliness which can be accomplished by the flesh apart from the Spirit. But the life of the resurrected glorified Lord is missing from all that. The veil must be removed and the hard heart must be broken before one can meet the living and abiding Word of God in His Glory.

The fourth thing we must notice is that the veil is removed only through Christ (v. 14). By this Paul indicates that the mysteries of God have not been permanently unveiled in such a way that they are now available to any who will approach the scriptures with the natural mind apart from the Spirit of God. If the mysteries were available to the natural mind, a "liberal" scholar would be an impossibility. Jesus, as the Word become flesh, could not be recognized as the Son of God by the scribes of His day apart from revelation. In His humanity He could only be recognized for who He was through the act of the Father's unveiling (Matt. 16:17). Jesus told the multitude which later deserted Him, "No one can come to me unless the Father who sent me draws him" (Jn. 6:44). So also the Word which has become Scripture cannot be seen in the fullness of His glory apart from the Father's unveiling. If those who were in the presence of the living Word in His incarnate form could not come to Him apart from the work of the Father, how much less can we come to Him through the mediation of the scriptures apart from the Father.

The Gospel is veiled to those who are perishing. "In their case the god of this world has blinded the minds of the unbelievers, to keep them from seeing the light of the gospel of the glory of Christ, who is the likeness of God" (II Cor. 4:4). Remembering that the larger context of this passage is the ministry of God's Word and the reading of the Bible, we recognize that the "god of this world" is none other than the humanistic god which challenged Adam to exalt his natural abilities to the position of deity. To the degree that one tries to justify himself before God on the basis of anything he has done or can do in the strength of his humanity, to that degree he is blinded to the light of the gospel. To the degree that one tries to unlock the secrets of the kingdom by his human knowledge of good and evil, to that degree he is trying to arrogantly exalt himself to the position of deity. But, "when a man turns to the Lord (as the only one who can do what needs to be done) then the veil is removed" (II Cor. 3:16).

Now, returning to our original question, "How does one receive with meekness the implanted Word?" we are ready to hear Paul's answer. "And we all, with unveiled face, beholding the glory of the Lord, are being changed into his likeness from one degree of glory to another; for this comes from the Lord who is the Spirit" (II Cor. 3:18). The purpose of the unveiling of the mind, then, is that we might be able to see the glory reflected there in the scriptures as it was on Moses' face. The glory reflected on Moses' face was a fading splendor. The glory of the Lord, which is "there" for those who read the scriptures in humility with unveiled faces, is an unfading splendor.

When we are seeking the "face of Christ" (II Cor. 4:6) rather than the reflection of our own human glory we begin to see something which is supernaturally imparted to us by the Lord who is the Spirit. We no longer see religious things, we see the glory of the eternal Word of God because we have turned to the Lord and away from ourselves.

This is a miracle. Just as the new birth is a miracle performed "from above" upon those who receive the Word by faith, so the miracle of the unveiled mind is performed "from above" upon those who turn to the Lord in meekness to receive the implanted Word by faith. It is a work of God's grace administered by the Lord who is the Spirit. Having begun by a work of the Spirit we must not try to continue by a work of the flesh. God's grace is not available to those who in their pride think they can accomplish the work by their natural abilities (Rom. 4:1-4).

This grace-work is not a once-for-all experience like the new birth. It is the daily miracle of walking by the Spirit in the life process of being changed into His likeness from one degree of glory to another. We cannot change ourselves into His likeness by any exercise of our human abilities. The verb "being changed" is passive. We do not change ourselves; He changes us as we behold His glory. The beholding is also from Him because it is

He who removes the veil. The removing of the veil is a work which God does for those who lay down their pride and take their position as humble recipients. "God opposes the proud but gives grace to the humble" (Jas. 5:5). This is not to say that there is nothing for us to do. In the next chapter we turn our attention to man's part which consists of getting himself in the proper position to receive the miracle.

9

MEEKNESS AND MIRACLES

Getting in the Right Place

In the preceding chapter we noticed that the work which needs to take place in our lives is a work which can only be accomplished by God. We can not change ourselves into His likeness. We will never become holy by our own efforts. Although this is a work of grace administered by the Spirit there are some things we can do to put ourselves in a position to be recipients of the miracle. In this chapter we turn our attention to man's part in the process of sanctification.

In positioning ourselves before Him we are not initiating the work of grace nor are we supplying any energy for its accomplishment. God remains sovereign. Like Zacchaeus, we can climb the tree, but it is Jesus who must give the invitation for us to come down and allow Him to enter our house (Lk. 19:5). We can only take our position and wait upon the Lord. This waiting is upon one who is faithful. "He who calls you is faithful, and he will do it" (I Thess. 5:24). The faithfulness promised in this verse is related to our theme of wholeness and sanctification.

The process of positioning ourselves before the faithful God in readiness to receive the miracle is outlined in several Old Testament passages. First let us look at the principle of the heart. "Keep your heart with all vigilance; for from it flows the springs of life" (Prov. 4:23). Whatever finds its way into our heart will manifest itself in our life. The heart is the base from which we operate. Our thinking, feeling and desiring (and from these our decisions and behavior) are determined by the formative "word" which rules in our heart. If our heart is ruled by a **false word** our feelings will be inappropriate, our thinking will be at variance with reality and our decisions will lead to vanity and striving after wind. But if the ruling word of our heart is the **living Word** of the living God our emotional responses will be proper, our thinking will reflect reality and our decisions will lead to the fullness of life on the highest plane.

The psalmist seems to have understood this. "I have laid up thy word in my heart, that I might not sin against thee" (Ps. 119:11). When the Word of God rules in a man's heart by the Spirit it brings deliverance from the bondages and sicknesses of the soul which hinder godly behavior. The Word in the heart brings freedom: "...where the Spirit of the Lord is, there is freedom" (II Cor. 3:17). It also brings wholeness and salvation to the soul. The life which springs from a heart ruled by the Word of God is a life of true rightenousness and holiness. The maturity of which we speak does not come by having passages of Scripture in the mind. It comes as the Word of the Lord is hidden in the **heart.** To the degree that this condition is fulfilled we will be able to "lead a life worthy of the Lord, fully pleasing to him, bearing fruit in every good work and increasing in the knowledge of God" (Col. 1:10).

How then do we hide the Word in our heart? The psalmist has provided some insights (Ps. 119:9-16). He begins by asking a question. "How can a young man keep his way pure?" We must also begin with this question. Until we are dissatisfied with our present level of development, recognizing our need for more purity, there will be no movement toward the next level of maturity. This dissatisfaction is what I was experiencing in Japan. I had come to the point of being fed up with the world with its bondages and false promises. Again in New Mexico it was the dissatisfaction with my inability to touch the realities of God through religious activities which brought me to recognize my need. I was fed up with religion apart from the real presence of the real God.

Next comes the answer: "...by guarding it according to thy word." This requires a comparing of the quality of our way of life with the life available through the Word. We must keep our lives "hemmed in" on all sides by the living Word of God. When the Spirit reveals an area of interest or an activity which falls short of the life available in Christ, the automatic response of the new man in Christ will be to seek God Himself, crying out, "Let me not wander from thy commandments!" (v. 10). Having thus taken our position in meekness under the Word of God, recognizing our need and its supply, crying out for help, we can now say, "Thy word have I hid in my heart..." (v. 11). After receiving the Word in this way we must still maintain an attitude of meekness. We must depend on the Lord to teach the meaning of His statutes (v. 12), because it is only those who are taught of God who come to the Lord (Jn. 6:45).

These two things, the **dissatisfaction** with things as they are and **seeing and receiving what is available** through the Word, keep us in a position of meekness under the Word. This meekness is not to be confused with feelings of condemnation or unworthiness. These only breed despair and depression. We speak here of the recognition of our constant need of the continuing work of God in our lives. Apart from His abiding presence we will never come to the point where we can be what He has called us to be. When this fact is seen in the context of His forgiveness and the availability of His presence it becomes "the power of God unto salvation" (Rom. 1:16). This recognition comes in the event of hearing the Word and taking our position in the meekness of faith under the revealed Word (Rom. 10:17).

There are those who have had the experience of the initial receiving of the Word in faith but who have not been able to grow in their ability to walk in that Word which they received. It is to this situation that the remaining steps in Psalm 119:13-16 are especially appropriate. Some response to the received Word is necessary. Zacchaeus had to come down from his sycamore tree and respond to Jesus' invitation before the reality of what God was doing in his life was manifested (Lk. 19:1-10). For the sake of simplicity we will study the needed responses under three categories: 1) Verbalizing, 2) Visualizing, and 3) Vitalizing.

These next steps will require a little more comment. The first thing is to **verbalize** the Word of God. As God begins to be the Teacher within a man's heart by the Spirit (Jn. 14:26), the new man must learn to say with the psalmist, "With my lips I declare all the ordinances of thy mouth" (Ps. 119:13). This simply means that we must learn to say what God says. "For a man believes with his heart and so is justified, and he confesses with his lips and so is saved" (Rom. 10:10). We must continue on to the maturity of salvation in the same way we began, i.e., **we must continue to direct the confession of our lips according to the Word of God.**

"A gentle (or wholesome) tongue is a tree of life, but perverseness in it breaks the spirit" (Prov. 15:4). A wholesome tongue is one which speaks from a heart which has received the Word of God with meekness thus allowing the tongue to speak accordingly. Perverseness is anything contrary to that Word. "Death and life are in the power of the tongue, and those who love it will eat its fruit" (Prov. 18:21). We can have a day of spiritual defeat by allowing our speech to be controlled by the word of the flesh, or we can have a day of feasting on the fruit of life if we allow the Word of God to control our tongue from the heart.

Next we notice that a condition of rejoicing comes when we enter into the **way** of His testimonies. "In the way of thy testimonies I delight as much as in all riches" (Ps. 119:14). The testimonies of God are the things He says in bearing witness to what He has made available for man through His mighty deeds. When we continue to repeat with our lips what God continues to say we will soon be in a position to see the work of the creative word of God in our life. The product of that creative work is related to **walking in the way of His testimonies.** This aspect of the process has to do with the category of "vitalizing" which we will take up next. Here we simply notice that, having learned to say what God says, we can begin to live in the reality of life on the highest plane. The only appropriate response to such a condition is "delight as much as in all riches."

The next thing which the psalmist mentions is meditation: "I will meditate on thy precepts, and fix my eyes on thy ways" (v. 15). In the Bible the word "meditation" refers to the practice of seeing or **visualizing** the Word and ways of God. The practice of meditating on the Word of God has fallen into disuse in many Christian communities. There are some who do not even know what meditation is, and others who are afraid of it because of certain "Eastern" practices. It is encouraging to notice that the tide is turning in our day, even though there are some excesses and misunderstandings as to how it should be practiced. This generation must set itself to work through the excesses in order to bring the art of meditation back into its rightful place among the list of Christian disciplines. **Meditation is a fixing of the eyes upon the ways and Word of God as outlined in the Scripture and unveiled by the Holy Spirit.** With eyes fixed upon the ways and Word of God we wait upon Him to remove the veil because it is only in this way that the Word comes to be in the heart as well as the mind.

The same principles can be seen in the instructions given to Joshua: "This book of the law shall not depart out of your mouth (i.e., say it with your mouth), but you shall meditate (i.e., fix your eyes) on it day and night, that you may be careful to do according to all that is written in it; for then you shall make your way prosperous, and then you shall have good success" (Josh. 1:8). **There is a relationship between what is received inwardly through meditation and what is performed outwardly.** In the psalm it was stated negatively: "that I might not sin against thee." Here it is stated positively: "that you may be careful to do according to all that is written." In both cases the relationship is clear. The practice of meditation coupled with speaking the Word is the process of hiding the Word in the heart. The result of having the Word in the heart is the ability to become a doer of the Word.

So as we receive the Word with meekness, hiding it in our heart through visualizing and verbalizing, we place ourselves in a position to experience the realities of what was seen in the removing of the veil. But this is not a magic formula. We cannot force the true God to move by practicing meditation and speaking words into the air. Any "god" which responds to meditation practiced for the purpose of manipulation would be the humanistic god of this world which establishes man in his flesh. This god, which is no god, is in conflict with the true God who requires the death of the old man. As death must precede resurrection, so the attitude of meekness and humility must precede true biblical meditation. One who would try to control God could never rightfully claim to be meek or humble.

But verbalizing and visualizing must never try to stand alone. We must also allow a **vitalizing.** Hearing the new Word from our new Father does not have its full effect in our lives until we begin to "act out" the Word, i.e., delighting in the **way** of His testimonies. Or, to say the same thing negatively, if we do not begin to see changes in our behavior we have not heard the omnipotent Word of God in faith. We have only touched the external logic of the human element. We have only received it as though it were the word of man. The word of man will never give us the ability to do the will of God. This insight does not relieve us of our responsibility to act in obedience to the Word. It does leave the initiative and power in the hands of God where it belongs.

Thus, the obedience of which we speak is not of the legalistic variety. It is a **rising up** to **BE** in **experience** what the **Father says we ARE** in **Christ Jesus.** It is an act of faith which finds its motive and its power in the covenant established in Him and applied through the Holy Spirit. This vitalizing takes place through recognition and acknowledgement. As we first **recognize** what has happened in Jesus Christ and then begin to **acknowledge** that work in our acts of gratitude and service we will discover the Holy Spirit's work in our lives. Teaching this concept in Idaho several years ago I made the statement, "We must act as though the Word of God is true even when we do not feel like it." Someone asked later if that was not encouraging hypocrisy. My response was a simple question: "If we really believe the Bible to be true is it not much more dishonest to act as though it were not true just because we don't have a certain feeling?" On the contrary, if we are not willing to act as though the Bible is true we expose the fact that we do not really believe it to be true.

Some examples and practical applications are in order here. Let us deal with forgiveness first. I am personally convinced that it is not possible to overcome the negative effect of the "word" we received from our earthly fathers until we have learned to forgive. **Forgiveness is in the beginning of God's work toward man and must be in the beginning of man's response to God.** "For if you forgive men their trespasses, your heavenly Father also will forgive you; but if you do not forgive men their trespasses, neither will your Father forgive your trespasses" (Mt. 6:14,15).

Forgiveness is more than verbalizing a word of affirmation toward the offending party. The parable of forgiveness in Matthew 18:23-25 is instructive. The basic elements of the parable are a king and two servants who owe debts. The first servant owes ten thousand talents (something like six million dollars). His debt is to the king. The second servant's debt is to the first servant amounting to one hundred denarii (roughly twelve dollars). Neither of these servants have the resources to pay the debt they owe.

The development of events within the parable is as follows: the first servant is called to account to the king and payment is demanded. When he asks for mercy the king forgave him all his debt. The first servant then encounters the second and demands payment. Unlike the king, however, the forgiven servant does not forgive his debtor but puts him in prison until he should pay. A report of this came to the king and he treated the first servant as he had treated his fellow. He put him in prison until he should pay all his debt.

It is clear that forgiveness in this parable means more than mere verbalization. Forgiveness means the release of the debtor from two aspects related to the debt. First there is the release from the **obligation** to pay. Then there is release from the threat of **penalty** for not paying. It is possible to say to someone, "That's O.K., you don't have to pay," but to begin to behave toward them in such a way that they are forced to pay the penalty for not paying. The closing statement of the parable shows that something needs to happen in the **heart** of the one who is forgiving. "So also will my Father do to each one of you (i.e., put you in the hands of the tormentors until you pay what you owe Him) unless you forgive your brother from your heart."

To make this practical, let us apply it to the situation of our earthly parents. Every father owes his son or daughter a measure of love and fatherly attention and every mother owes her children a measure of love and motherly attention. These are legitimate debts. No one would consider a child to be unreasonable who thinks his father and mother should love him. To see the implications of this it might be helpful to see ourselves as holding an I.O.U. for every unit of love and affection which we should have received from our parents but did not. The I.O.U. is duly signed and notarized. It is not morally wrong to expect payment.

Our King has forgiven us our debt of sin which we were totally unable to pay and He has released us from the threat of having to pay the penalty for our nonpayment. In this freedom we might come to think that many of the problems we have in life are a result of being deprived of love by our parents. Whether our thinking is correct on this point or not this puts us in the place of the servant who "meets" his debtor on the way from the king. If we do not forgive our parents at this "meeting" then we have chosen to be identified with the unforgiving servant who put his debtor in prison for nonpayment.

If we think of the bars of this prison as breaches in relationship then two insights emerge. First we recognize that there are many walls and barriers which separate fathers from sons and sons from fathers, daughters from mothers and sisters from brothers. Even though we may be in the same room they cannot come to us and we cannot go to them because of the hurt which has come between us as bars. We have in fact put one another in prison. The second thing we notice is that the torment in our lives is not because our parents did not love us but **because we have not**

forgiven them for not loving us. Our King has put us in the hands of the tormentors until we should pay all our debt.

We may not be able to identify the "jailers" but it seems the parable is saying that some of the difficulties and struggles within our lives may be a result of unforgiveness in our hearts. Since the unforgiveness is in the **heart** we are not always consciously aware of it as such. Recently I was counselling with a young lady who had a serious food disorder which was a combination of anorexia, bulimia and food allergies. In the course of our discussion she became aware of some hidden resentments against her mother. I led her through the exercise of forgiveness which we will describe shortly and she was healed of her eating problem including the allergies. The "word" of her mother which had been a formative element in her disorder no longer held her captive because she had forgiven her mother.

Here is how it works. See yourself as the servant who has been forgiven but who has refused to forgive the "other" (whether that be your father, mother or some friend). Do not do this in some general way but think of some specific instance where the "other" should have loved you in some very specific way but failed to do so. **Recognize** yourself as that one who has been placed in the hands of the jailer because of your unforgiveness in that specific situation. This is an act of guarding your heart according to the Word. Then **acknowledge** your unforgiveness to God. This begins the process of actualizing or vitalizing the Word. These steps are derived from an understanding of Psalms 32:3-5.

When I declared not my sin, my body wasted away
     through my groaning all day long.
For day and night thy hand was heavy upon me:
     my strength was dried up as by the heat of summer.
I acknowledged my sin to thee,
     and did not hide my iniquity;
I said, "I will confess my transgression to the Lord";
     then thou didst forgive the guilt of my sin.

At this point I have found it very effective to encourage people to see themselves in a cell block where the ones whom they have not forgiven are behind bars. There you are with a piece of paper in your hand which read, "I.O.U. twenty units of fatherhood" (or motherhood or friendship etc.). In the other hand you have the key to unlock the cells. Now understand this. If we were dealing with money, forgiveness of the debt would mean setting the person free not to pay and releasing him from the penalty of nonpayment. If you try to demand something to compensate for your loss it is not forgiveness. Forgiveness means tearing up the I.O.U. and releasing the debtor from prison.

In your mind's eye tear up the piece of paper and say to your debtor, "I set you free not to pay; you don't have to love me." Then go over to the cell, take the key, unlock the door and give them their liberty. This is something which you do before God as an act of obedience. In this act we become like our heavenly Father in His willingness to forgive with no expectation of return. Do not necessarily expect your debtor to change in any way. This is between you and your King.

Now Jesus will be there to meet you and minister to your needs. Turn to Him. Let Him know that your "emotional ledger" is not a balanced account. You are "in the red" as far as love is concerned. Since you did not receive the love which your debtor owed you, you are now twenty units short with no hope of recovering those units now that you have torn up the I.O.U. and released the debtor from prison. This leaves you in a condition of being unable to show love and affection in an effective way to your creditors, i.e., your own children, spouse or parents. It is as though your heart was broken when you were rejected or slighted by the one upon whom you depended for love. Now whatever love you may have received has leaked out and now you have difficulty giving and receiving love.

> The Spirit of the Lord God us upon me,
>> because the Lord has anounted me
>> to bring good tidings to the afflicted;
> He sent me to bind up the brokenhearted,
>> to proclaim liberty to the captives,
>> and the opening of the prison
>> to those who are bound. (Isa. 61:1)

There is clearly a relationship between the broken heart and certain bondages and afflictions. Simply ask the Lord Jesus to bind up your broken heart and wait quietly for Him to do that inner work. Then ask Him to cause His love to be shed abroad in your heart through the Holy Spirit (Rom. 5:5) so that you may be able to love others as He has loved you. Then begin to look for opportunities to behave in a loving way toward those He brings into your life. Allow your life to be **vitalized** by the love of God.

A second example of vitalizing will be offered from Hebrews 12:3-16. This passage begins with an exhortation to consider Jesus in His situation of enduring the hostility of sinners against Himself. The word "consider" here does not merely imply intellectual exercise but a considering with a view to coming to have a life style which reflects that which is seen. This "considering" with a view to "becoming" is designed to bring us to a place where we will "not grow weary or fainthearted" (v.3). How often we become weary when others are continually expressing hostility toward us! How easy it is to grow fainthearted in our attempt to respond to hostility in a spirit of meekness! We usually either draw back into our "closet" or begin to counter with hostility ourselves.

What do we discover when we consider Jesus? I see a man who is at peace with God and at peace with Himself. When others attack Him or fail to show Him due respect it does not evoke a response of anger or uncover hidden resentments. He has no T-shirt to hide and no sin to cover. When they put Him on the cross I see only compassion and forgiveness for those who are expressing the ultimate hostility and rejection against Him. The more they press Him the more love flows forth. He resisted the human tendency to become hostile in return. He experienced the ultimate struggle against the inclination to defend Himself and prove Himself right and worthy of acceptance. In His struggle against sin (not in others but in Himself) His blood was shed. He chose rather to die than to fight back or defend Himself and His rights.

With this consideration of Jesus in mind the Hebrew writer said, "In your struggle against sin you have not yet resisted to the point of shedding your blood" (v. 4). Each of us has a "boiling point'' beyond which we no longer resist the sin of anger and hostility toward those who do not give us the honor we think we deserve. Some take longer to boil than others but none of us have resisted this tendency to the point of choosing death rather than hostility. Those who are more outwardly hostile try to be the jailer in the prison who makes the debtor pay by inflicting pain. In others the hostility takes a more subtle form which is called passive resistance. We crawl into our closets and give the silent treatment. This is the sin of sending our debtors to prison by depriving them of our fellowship. None of us have given ultimate resistance to this sin within ourselves.

At this point the text makes a curious turn. The apostle reminds us that God has addressed us as sons:

My son, do not regard lightly the discipline of
the Lord, nor lose courage when you are punished
by him. For the Lord disciplines him whom he loves
and chastises every son whom he receives.

Then we are told that ''it is for discipline that we have to endure'' (vv. 5-7). Although it may appear that the writer has changed topics from the hostility of sinners to a discussion of discipline we must realize that the two are related in his mind. It is for discipline and training that we have to endure the hostility of sinners who come against us. God is treating us as sons by bringing situations into our lives which give us an opportunity to ''share in his holiness'' (v. 10).

God's holiness here must not be understood abstractly. It is related to the self-emptying work of Jesus Christ which manifested the extent of God's love for His creation. It is the holiness of His love and mercy which we are called to share. As we lay down our self-life in the face of hostility, forgiving the offender, we actively participate in the holiness and righteousness of God. When we turn the other cheek we behave like God did in Christ Jesus. When we go the extra mile with a hostile sinner we are doing what God has done for us in Christ Jesus. When we give our cloak to the one who is suing us for our coat we become like Him in true righteousness and holiness. In short, we allow our life to be **vitalized** by the Word of God rather than the word of man.

"For the moment all discipline seems painful rather than pleasant;" the passage in Hebrews continues, "later it yields the peaceful fruit of righteousness to those who have been trained by it" (v. 11). Those who do not submit to the training which the Lord offers in the situation of the hostile sinner will only experience the pain of the discipline. They will never see the joy and peace which come on the other side of the cross where the resurrection is a reality. The discipline is painful and it takes time. Don't expect to be an accomplished expert in God's holiness without pain and don't expect it after the first experience. Be willing to go through that again. Looking to the joy which is before you, endure the cross (v. 2).

The most common reason for failure to encounter the hostility of sinners in a manner consistent with the holiness of God's love is that we misunderstand how one should pray in the situation. The issue is clarified as we see the implications of verse 15, "See to it that no one fail to obtain the grace of God; that no 'root of bitterness' spring up and cause trouble..." This phrase "fail to obtain" in the New Testament times was a banking term which is roughly equivalent to our phrase "insufficient funds." It is as though we write a check on our "grace account" when we are faced with a hostile sinner. As the situation develops the check bounces and we blow our cool or walk away in anger thus failing to obtain the grace of God which was needed in the situation.

Here is how it usually goes. The hostile sinner begins his attack and we size up the situation; "This case will require about twenty units of grace," we think. So we pray, "Lord give me twenty measures of grace to get through this situation." The hostility of the sinner continues to increase. We hold our peace (at least externally) as long as we can. But the hostility eventually mounts to the point where our "grace check" bounces. The problem is not that we did not request enough grace; nor is it that God is not making enough grace available. **The problem is that we are writing our check on the wrong account.**

The fact is that our Father has granted to each of His children two separate grace accounts. One is His grace toward us, the other is His grace in us for others. In our self-centeredness we fail to recognize that the hostile sinner is very much in need of God's grace. In our self-righteousness we ask for grace to get through the situation in such a way that we will appear to be some sort of super saint. Often our thinking is that if we can keep calm in the situation the hostile sinner will be exposed for what he is and everyone will think we are wonderful. We ask for grace to use it for our own self-centeredness. Is it any wonder that God does not give us grace to exalt ourselves at the expense of the other person! God resists the proud and exalts the humble.

When we pray, "God give me grace in this hostile situation," I believe that He does give us enough grace to accomplish His will in the situation. But the grace is placed in the account of grace in us for others. If we allow the discipline of the Lord to get our attention away from ourselves we would notice that it is the hostile sinner who is in need of grace. Jesus did not merely pray that He might receive grace to endure the cross. His heart went out in compassion for the ones who were abusing Him and failing to give Him the honor due Him. "Father forgive them they know not what they do," was His prayer. If we could learn to say, "Father, this person who is pressing me really has a burden, would you give me the grace to bear his burden," then our grace checks would not bounce.

In this way we become not mere hearers of the Word but doers. As we delight in the doing of it the new Word of our new Father is not merely accepted as an external article of clothing which might cover our bad self-image but it is imparted to our very being. We begin to experience the reality of being changed into His likeness from one degree of glory to another. As we willingly take the position of meekness before God and humility before our fellow-man we begin to be like Him who "counted not equality with God a thing to be held on to" (Phil. 2:4). It is in this way that we participate in His holiness: the holiness of His love.

The attitude of meekness is a necessary element in receiving the Word. We must take our position under the Word of God

recognizing that apart from Him we can do nothing (Jn. 15:5).
For thus says the high and lofty One, who inhabits
eternity, whose name is Holy; "I dwell in the high
and holy place, and also with him who is of a contrite
and humble spirit, to revive the spirit of the humble,
and to receive the heart of the contrite." (Isa. 57:15)

The Word of God can be a creative element in the life of man
only when it is received with meekness. When that Word is
received (as the T-shirt was received to produce the self-image)
it will come as the living and active Word of God and produce
the image and likeness of God in man. This takes time and is
sometimes painful, but it is the power of God unto salvation for
those who believe (Rom. 1:16) and who present their bodies as
living sacrifices so that they may be living examples of the will
of God in the earth (Rom. 12:1-2).

In the next chapter we will focus our attention on the dangers
of trying to superimpose our personal god-image over the True
God. We will see that this is what we are really doing when we
try to manipulate Him into doing our will rather than responding
to His Word. There are no steps of action which man can take
in human wisdom or by human strength which will in any way
put God under obligation. The only step of action needed is a
step which God has already taken and continues to take. Man
can receive the benefit of that act only as he takes his position
in meekness before God under His living and active Word and
begins to love his neighbor as himself.

10

THE GOD WHO IS

Destroying False Images

In our first chapter we raised four basic questions which we must always be asking ourselves as we travel on our journey into wholeness. For the sake of review and in preparation for the material in this chapter we will present those questions again: 1) Where did I come from? 2) Where am I going or what am I becoming? 3) What is this "world" all about and how do things work? and, 4) What or who is my source of strength and direction?

Now, again for the sake of preparation, let us review the answers which have been suggested. First is the question of **whence.** We found two answers: 1) Our human nature is derived from Adam by **generation** and has been separated from its original life source in God, but 2) those who are born from above have received a new nature which comes from God by **regeneration.** Second is the question of **whither.** It is related to the first. Our destiny is determined by the potential of the seed which produced us. Here also we found two answers: 1) Our human nature is destined to **death and separation,** but 2) our new nature is destined to be conformed to the image of Jesus Christ and to reign with

Him in life. Third is the question of **where,** not in the sense of geographic location, but with a view to how things "work" and how we are to behave ourselves here. We noticed that our ideas of the world and how we fit in 1) were influenced by the **word** received in childhood and 2) they can begin to be influenced by the **Word of God.** Fourth is the question of **God.** Again we have noticed two things: 1) there is a "god" of this world who establishes man in his human resistance against the true God, and 2) there is the eternal God who is both Creator and Savior— who makes Himself and His life available to those who deny themselves to follow the leading of His Holy Spirit.

From the beginning we have said that it is our images of reality which effect the way we think and respond in any given situation. Our conception (or image) of the world and its laws of operation will determine our expectations. What we expect also has an effect upon what we are able to see. The three basic images which effect our "seeing" are the self-image, our world-image, and our image of God. Our concentration so far has been upon the self-image and its development, although we have occasionally mentioned the other two. It now remains for us to give more serious attention to the others, especially to the image of God.

As preliminary definitions we will simply suggest that the world-image is our conception of what is "out there" in the natural world, e.g., the forces which oppose us and how they can be avoided or conquered, and the things which give us pleasure and how they can be received. The God-image is our conception of what (or who) is ultimate in dignity, power and authority to give aid or to oppose us in our attempt to accomplish our goals in life. To make our point in the form of a question we may ask: to what or to whom must we render ultimate respect and honor? Before what or whom must we stand in unqualified fear? From what or whom can we expect an unchangeable curse or blessing?

Some illustration is needed to clarify the issues. While I was a student at the University of New Mexico, I was on the intramural wrestling team. Without being conscious of it, I saw myself as a loser (self-image). I saw my opponent as much bigger and much more experienced (world-image). God was not even an issue because, in my view, He was only "there" on Sunday and was only interested in what happened in the church building. This exposes the fact that my "god" was really no god at all. I had more respect for my opponent than I did for the God I worshiped on Sunday. With "li'l ol' me" coming up against that huge giant of a man with all that experience in battle, and with "no-god" to help me, who could expect me to win? It is as though I saw my life as a series of contests in which I play the role of the loser. My place in the world was to provide someone for all those "winners" to defeat.

Those were the images which were influencing my performance at that time. The first thing wrong is that my opponent and I had both been weighed prior to the match; we were both the same size. The second thing wrong, which I learned later, is that he was also fighting in his first match; we had the same level of experience. He was an experienced giant only in my imagination. But when the opportunity came for me to gain the advantage, since I could not conceive of myself as having any advantage, I hesitated and lost. I was defeated by my imagination before the starting bell was sounded.

I was also lifting weights in those days. My trainer suggested that I enter the state weight-lifting contest. I saw myself as the "ninety-eight pound weakling" who was pictured in the barbell advertisements. I knew all the other contestants would be huge, barrel-chested men with the classical physique of the Greek gods. I could just see myself on the stage dropping the bar and a large crowd of people laughing while my opponent came to lift with one arm what I had failed to lift with two. The laughing crowd and the strong opponent were all a part of my world-image at that time.

I gave some silly excuse as to why I would not be interested. My insecurities (caused by the images) kept me from entering the contest but I did attend as a spectator. To my amazement the young man who won the first place in my weight class did so with about two pounds less than I could lift. I may not have won the contest even if I had entered. The images have a way of influencing behavior in such a way as to prove themselves true.

I would probably have found a way to lift less weight and yet appear (even to myself) to be doing my best. Because of the images beneath the surface, I would have to lose in one way or another. I had to fulfill my function in life as a loser.

The issues in these examples are not of earth shattering significance. My success or failure as a person is not bound up with winning or losing contests. The point here is that one's images of himself and his world do have an effect upon his performance. The effect of these images is not always negative. In some cases they may have a very positive effect. One with a more aggressive nature who thinks of himself as weak may put forth greater effort to overcome his weakness. This extra effort could bring him to the point of having mastery over one who is actually stronger. Although it might cause him to become a winner, his image of himself as weak will have been an influential element in his performance.

Before we continue, let us recall that the images are related to the "word" we received from the important others in our lives during those formative years. It is difficult to see beyond those images. Once I had received the image of the dumb-dumb, it was hard to accept any evidence to the contrary. Once I had received an image of the world as hostile, it was difficult to see anything other than giants and walled cities. My life was dominated by those images.

Whatever may be "out there" in the real world, we view our world through the word we received about that world. We tend to see what we expect to see and we expect to see what the received word has prepared us to see. For example, if a man has received a word which says, "wives are hostile," then it will be difficult for him to see anything but hostility in his wife, no matter how gentle she may have appeared before they were married. He did not see hostility in her before they were married because she was not yet a wife. The word he received had not prepared him to see hostility in pretty little unmarried girls. That may also be the reason why he continues to see the unmarried girls around him as more desirable than his wife. But if he divorces his wife to marry another, he will very likely find his new wife to be just as hostile as his first. What we see "out there" is highly influenced by the expectations created by the word-images we have received.

The old images can be defused or destroyed and new ones can be formed if a new word comes which is strong enough to overpower the old word and capture the imagination. The extent and value of the change is dependent upon the nature and the source of the new word as well as the level of our faith in (or receiving of) the new word. A man might be able to make a complete break from the traditions of his fathers and from the vain way of his early training if he leaves the "farm" of his childhood and receives the word of the "city dwellers" of adult life. This change is only superficial, however, because the word of the city is of human origin as surely as is the word of the farm.

The only source which can cause any basic changes in our nature is God Himself. As He speaks His Word by His Spirit the Word comes with all the resources of God to accomplish its intended purpose. We experience the reality of the living and active Word as we receive it with meekness, as we take our position under the Word rather than placing ourselves over it as judges. When He says that we are "more than conquerors through him who loved us" (Rom. 8:37), and when we receive that word by faith and begin to say what God says, then we enter into the process of becoming more than conquerors in our experience from one degree of reality to another. As we learn to say in faith, "I am what God says I am in this world," our self-image and our world-image will begin to take shape according to the Word of God.

Turning now to the more serious matter of the image of God, the question might be raised: "What would have happened if I had approached those contests with a different concept of God?" Suppose I had entered that wrestling match with an image of God as one who would never allow me to lose. I might have gone much farther with that image than I did with the one I had. Sooner or later, however, there would have been another wrestler who believed that God would not allow him to lose either. Then what? If I had won, should I conclude that God loves me more than my opponent? Or that perhaps my God was stronger than his God? If I lost would that mean that God had abandoned me?

This kind of questioning leads into a blind alley. Rather than trying to deal with hypothetical situations, let us consider an actual situation as it is presented in the Bible (read Josh. 5:13-15). After successfully leading the people of Israel across the Jordan, Joshua was walking near Jericho at night. He was probably considering various battle plans against the first walled city in the land. Suddenly, there was a man standing before him with his drawn sword in his hand. Like any good military man, Joshua immediately challenged him and demanded that he identify himself.

"Are you for us or for our adversaries?" With this the battle line was clearly drawn. If the man with the drawn sword is on the Israelites' side then Joshua could relax. But if he is for the people of Jericho, he would have a conflict on his hands.

"No," the man's answer came with profound implications, "but as commander of the army of the Lord I have now come." We will paraphrase this answer to catch the significance of what he said. "Joshua, I have not come to take sides; I have come to take over. I have not come to honor the battle lines as you have drawn them; I have come to do battle with those who are my adversaries. I have come as Lord to see that my will is accomplished in the earth. Now, Joshua, whether I am for you or for your adversaries depends on your response to my Lordship. Take off your shoes, this place is sanctified by my presence."

The commander of the army of the Lord, who was none other than the Lord Himself (otherwise He would not have commanded Joshua to worship Him), proceeded to outline an extraordinary battle plan for the conquering of Jericho. Joshua and his men executed the plan, marching around the city once each day for six days and seven times on the seventh day. After the final round they shouted, the walls fell down, and a great victory was wrought for Israel that day.

That was not the operation of an image of God having its influence from beneath the level of human consciousness. That was God manifesting Himself as Lord. The victory did not come because of Joshua's ability to capture the imagination of his troops with some sensational idea of what God might do. The power of positive thinking, valuable though it may be, does not cause stone walls which are fourteen feet thick to crumble to the ground. The God who is the true God made His lordship known in that event.

Yahweh (Jehovah), The God of Israel, is not a God who is formed in the people's imagination through the preaching of some charismatic leader with superior religious instincts. God is not the work of man's hands nor is He the creation of man's imagination. The Lord is God. He has formed heaven and earth and all that is in them. This God does not allow Himself to be restricted by an image of man's making, whether that image be in man's mind of worked into wood or stone. According to Jeremiah, those who make and worship such images, "have inherited nought but lies, worthless things in which there is no profit. Can a man make for himself gods? Such are no gods!" (Jer. 16:19,20).

The story of the next battle in the book of Joshua demonstrates the futility of following a concept (image) of God. After defeating Jericho, Joshua gave orders to go up against the next city, Ai. It is obvious that his instructions were influenced by an image of God which had been established in the minds of all the people by the success of crossing over Jordan and the overwhelming victory over Jericho. He certainly had no word of instruction from the Lord as he had had for Jericho.

"Let not all the people go up," the spies suggested, "but let about two or three thousand men go up and attack Ai; do not make the whole people toil up there, for they are but few" (Josh. 7:3). The world-image operating here is something like: "Those few little insignificant people up there in that li'l ol' city." The God-image which influenced their thinking was: "The Almighty is with us and against our adversaries." And the self-image is something like: "With this God on our side we can conquer anything."

Their thinking is logical enough, and they surely had no trouble capturing the imagination of the troops, not after Jericho.

The God who had delivered that city into their hands with such a miraculous demonstration of power would have no trouble with a little village like Ai. But Joshua and his men were operating under a false assumption, i.e., that the God who was with them at Jericho would automatically be with them at Ai. When they launched the attack they were defeated. The image of "God-with-us" was highly charged, and even had a historical confirmation, but it was not strong enough to defeat "li'l ol' Ai" since God Himself was not with them. This incident revealed something about the "commander of the army of the Lord" which Joshua had not noticed.

After this defeat Joshua prayed, "...why hast thou brought this people over the Jordan at all, to give us into the hands of the Amorites, to destroy us?"

"Arise, why have you thus fallen on your face?" The Lord's reply was to the point; it was not time to pray, it was time to act. "Israel has sinned; they have transgressed my covenant which I commanded them...**I will be with you no more,** unless you destroy the devoted things from among you" (Josh. 7:6-12, emphasis mine).

This explains the response of the man with the drawn sword when Joshua had challenged him earlier. The reason his answer came as a simple "no" (rather than committing himself to Joshua or to his adversaries) is because God's commitment to man is never a blank check. God does not make Himself or His army available to defend the battle line as it is established by man. Sometimes He strengthens the enemy against His people. The commander has His own battle plan, and He draws the line. His "armies" march against covenant disloyalty before they march against the adversaries of heathenism. Judgment sometimes begins at the house of the Lord (I Pet. 4:17).

Our point here is that Joshua planned the attack against Ai under the influence of a false image of God. This "God-is-with-us-no-matter-what" image was obviously false as far as the attack against Ai was concerned. It was a delusion (based solidly on something which God had actually done but, nevertheless, delusion). Their delusion was in thinking that God was somehow committed to repeat His Jericho performance. Since the God who is the real God did not honor what the army was trying to do at Ai it is safe to assume that Joshua was following his own human heart rather than God as he gave instructions to attack Ai. (The word "heart" is used here to refer to that "place" within man from which the images have their influence.)

Joshua discovered, as many of us have, that God has not obligated Himself to conform His activities to our preconceived notions of what He ought to do. The name by which He identified Himself to Moses was "I AM WHO I AM," or as the margin has it, "I WILL BE WHAT I WILL BE" (Ex. 3:14). By this name He has identified Himself as Lord over Himself in the sense that He has reserved for Himself the right to be whatever He wants to be in any given situation. Joshua's frustration and defeat at Ai came as a result of making battle plans based on false expectations concerning what God might do. At worst he expected that God would leave them to fight the battle on their own. He never suspected that the God who had crumbled the walls of Jericho might actually strengthen the enemies against them. But He did!

At some early stage in our lives we all receive some "word" about God which forms an image in our heart. It seems that the natural human thing to do at that age is to accept the image as an accurate representation of God Himself just as we received our image of ourselves and of the world without serious questioning. It would appear that man was originally designed (created) to receive images of himself, of the world and of God through the spoken and enacted Word. And it would appear that God, in creating man with this inclination, intended for his thoughts, emotions and behavior to be influenced by the Word received in meekness.

The problem is that, since the fall of Adam, the word that a child receives about himself, the world and God is a word of man rather than the Word of God. As long as that God-image is tested only in the "believing" community, the child can grow and develop his concept of God in the confines of his delusion. If he never goes beyond his little community he may even remain faithful to his delusion even unto death.

The God who **IS**, however, has a way of bringing us into crisis situations, forcing us to choose between Himself and our images, as He did with Joshua. In the crisis we discover that our image of God cannot save us or give us life. When we have received a concept of God apart from the revelation of the true God, we have received "naught but lies, worthless things in which there is no profit" (Jer. 16:19). These concepts are worthless and empty even if they are based on something which God has actually done or said. Why should we expect anything but frustration and defeat when the God-image which we follow is one of the no-gods of which Jeremiah spoke? When this "god" in whom we put our trust disappoints us, we come to a crossroad in our journey. At this point we must—we will—make a decision about God, and that decision will determine the road we take from there.

One road leads to an atheistic stance which says, "Since my god has not proven himself to be God, there must be no God." It is often true enough that the god in whom we trust does not really exist outside of the imaginations of our heart. When a false image of God is shattered, however, it does not necessarily follow that there is no true God. When Bertrand Russel's article, "Why I am Not a Christian" first came to my attention I could not help but think that, if real Christianity were as he described it, I would not be a christian either. The god which he denied is the no-god created by the imagination of man. The "Christ" which he rejected is one of the many antichrists who have come into the world through human speculation (I Jn. 2:18). In refusing to acknowledge as God that which is false and empty, one does not dispose of the God who IS.

The second road one might choose leads to the religiosity against which Bertrand Russel spoke. When the god in whom we trust does not do things our way, we might refuse to believe that the crisis is real. By denying the reality we can establish the god of our imagination. This denial can be accomplished in several ways.

In order to save our god we might build a strong political structure within our churches to enforce the rules of our god. These rules can be enforced by the ultimate sanction—excommunication from the "people of god" (which is so much as to say "ourselves"). When certain people claim to be receiving real life from God in a way which is not consistent with our image of God we can convince ourselves and our people that they are deceived. After all, we say to ourselves, they cannot really be receiving from God since they are not a part of our group and don't do things the way we do.

Or we might engage in mental gymnastics to formulate doctrines to defend our god from the logical attacks of those who are not a part of our group. When others try to convince us that we are following a delusion, presenting evidence from their own experience which indicates that they have touched the realities of God, we can hide behind our doctrinal walls. We can comfort ourselves with the thought that, although they may be receiving blessings in this life, we will have the blessings of the life to come. Those who are our doctrinal adversaries could never participate in those future blessings since they are not a part of our group and do not have the truth. So we go blindly on our way clinging to our god which is no god.

We might even become very aggressive in our "faith." With this faith of ours we might accomplish great things for ourselves in terms of wealth, fame or success in this world. But the god which we defend, and through which we work mightily, might still be the no-god of human imagination. There are powers available to the psyche of man which can work wonders and signs. The "power of positive thinking", for example, is a real power which can accomplish great things for the man who gives himself to that power. But this power can be related to the true God only to the degree that a man's thinking is determined by the Word of God. If we have a "god" which is available to us to accomplish our human goals apart from the guidance of the Holy Spirit, it is not the God of Abraham, Isaac and Jacob whom we serve.

One of the problems of this religious path is that there are occult and psychic resources available to man by which he can establish his human god. When we set ourselves to a task with sufficient human aggressiveness we might be able to "prove" that our god is with us even while the true God is against us. We may be able to gain enough influence to dominate others, and we may present our political power as evidence that God is one our side. We may produce logical and systematic teachings which can convince the human intellect (especially those who already believe what we believe), and we may offer these products of our intellect as proof that God has given us wisdom and understanding beyond our peers. We may even have a ministry with ''signs following'' and view those signs as an indication that God has made His powers available to us.

As we go our own way in the name of the Lord, we often interpret every obstacle as the resistance of evil men or as the work of the devil. We seldom stop to consider that the true God might be trying to get our attention. After all, He is the one we think we are defending. In the face of opposition from the true God, we may increase our political pressure, study harder, or try to increase the power of our faith by ''believing against and in spite of'' the opposition. Like Balaam we press forward in our rebellion, standing against god's resistance to our movement, and blame the ''donkeys'' around us for the problems we are having (Num. 22:23). It would be too strong a blow to our pride to admit that the god who is with us is the no-god of human imagination. It would be too humiliating for us to consider that the power source which we are plugged into is the power of the human psyche or perhaps even demonic. Those who continue in this way may someday hear Jesus say, ''I never knew you; depart from me, you evil doers'' (Matt. 7:33).

If we have a god who will defend our human position, no matter what, he is not the One who met Joshua in the night by Jericho. If we have a god who will support our human strength and fulfill our human vision, it is not the God who allowed the Israelite army to be defeated at Ai. If we have a god who is impressed with our human wisdom and who needs our logical defense, it is not the God of Paul who destroys the wisdom of the wise. ''God chose what is weak in the world to shame the strong, God chose what is low and despised in the world, even the things that are not, to bring to nothing things that are, so that no human being might boast in the presence of God" (I Cor. 1:27-29).

The third alternative at the crossroad of crisis is a road which few are willing to travel. It is the way which allows the true God to manifest Himself as the God He IS without any need for human definition or defense. This stance allows God Himself to choose how He will express His divinity in each situation. On this road man takes a position in the crisis which can say, "If he is a god, let him contend for himself, because his altar has been torn down" (Judg. 6:31).

This puts us in a vulnerable position if we are trying to establish ourselves in this world as men of God. It takes more real faith to allow God to prove Himself than it does to take a firm position for the god created by man's imagination. This is so because there is no guarantee that He will manifest Himself in such a way as to prove to our friends and opponents that He is what we have said He is. Even if we have represented Him accurately, His act might take some form which our friends and opponents would not recognize as such. True faith always leaves man's humanity in a vulnerable position. It was so with Jesus on the cross, and it will be so with those who follow Him. But, in allowing our humanity to be in that position, we allow God to prove Himself in His own way. "I will all the more gladly boast of my weaknesses," Paul said, "that the power of Christ may rest upon me" (II Cor. 12:9).

We have learned that many of the frustrations we encounter on our journey are a direct result of our inappropriate images of self, of the world and of God. We find ourselves in difficult situations because we expect the world (and sometimes even God) to be conformed to our images. We try to adjust our behavior according to what we think the world expects of us in the role we have unconsciously chosen for ourselves, and we are surprised (if not swept away) when the world does not seem to respond as we had expected. If God is an issue in our decisions, we try to live according to what we think He expects of us, and we are devastated when He does not hold up His end of our bargain. Unfortunately, when things go wrong we try to change our world and our god to conform to our images rather than adjusting our images. Things only get worse.

Most of us have probably had many trials which would not have been necessary if we had judged ourselves and our world differently. If we had been more sensitive to the God who IS, our lives might have been less complicated. There would still be struggles, no doubt, but there would be less anxiety because the burden of success would be upon His shoulders instead of ours. Our conflicts would be with His adversaries rather than with Him, and we would fight those battles in the power of His might instead of in our own human strength. Who knows where we might end up in this journey if we could learn to follow God rather than trying to lead Him!

Bell bows down, Nebo stoops,
    their idols are on beasts and cattle;
these things you carry are loaded
    as burdens on weary beasts.
They stoop, they bow down together,
    they cannot save the burden,
    but themselves go into captivity.
Hearken to me, O house of Jacob,
    all the remnant of the house of Israel,
who have been borne by me from your birth,
    carried from the womb;
even to your old age I am He,
    and to gray hairs I will carry you.
I have made, and I will bear;
    I will carry and will save. (Isa. 46:1-4)

11

ON TO MATURITY

Obedience to the Truth

Our purpose has been to trace the various stages of the development of the self-image, to show the way out of the bondages of the old adamic nature and to indicate the way of freedom available to the new man in Christ. We discovered that one's self-image is related to a word received in childhood and confirmed through the process of growing up within the community. We also noticed that one's self-image is related to how he conceives himself within the context of his world-image. For example, during my short-lived wrestling career I thought of myself as a loser whose existence was justified by being available for the winners to defeat. This relationship between the self-image and the world-image is so close that the self-image might be referred to more accurately as the "who-I-am-in-this-world-image."

When we come to show the way out, we indicated that there is no way out apart from being born anew and receiving with meekness the implanted Word of God. The **reality** of "who-I-am-in-this-world" is **radically altered** when we are born of God. The actuality of the change is often not immediately manifested in the way we act in this world because it takes time for us to become fully aware of our new self (notice, we are not saying, "self-image", because this is no mere image of the self. This is the true self). As this awareness grows, we begin to receive the new Word from our new Father. Then we discover that our new self is more related to Jesus Christ than it is to this world as we conceive it. This relationship is so close that the new self could be referred to more accurately as "who-I-am-in-Christ."

The first "who-I-am" was born of Adam and is related to the world as it is viewed through the eyes of man's fallen nature. The second "who-I-am" is born of God and is related to Christ as He is viewed through the eyes of His Father. The Father's view of His Son is presented in Scripture in such a way as to be available for the "many sons" who are being brought to glory (Heb. 2:10). As these many sons hear and receive the Father's view they are brought into ever increasing health and wholeness of the soul.

In chapters eight and nine we outlined the principles by which this Word might be received and incorporated into life. Chapter ten was inserted as a warning against trying to force God to fit into the patterns of our preconceived notions. We tried to make it clear that we must worship and serve the true God rather than an image of God.

The springboard for the final step of our journey together will be a statement which Peter made in the context of his statement that we are born of the Word of God. "Having purified your souls by your obedience to the truth for a sincere love of the brethren, love one another earnestly from the heart" (I Pet. 1:22). The "purifying of the soul" is related to the process which we earlier called the salvation of the soul. The purpose of this purifying process is "for a sincere love of the brethren." Without this purifying we will never be able to exercise that love of God which has been "poured into our hearts through the Holy Spirit" (Rom. 5:5). Without this purifying our love of the brethren will never be sincere. It will only be a cover for our self-seeking motivations. Pure behavior can only come from a pure soul. The center of man (which is responsible for the behavior of man) must be purified.

Our interest here is in the phrase "obedience to the truth." The curious thing about this phrase is that we do not normally think of "truth" as something to be obeyed. It is something to be understood or learned. The word translated "truth" (*alethia*) is a negative word meaning something like "un-secret", "un-concealed", or "un-veiled." This reminds us of the concept of the removing of the veil which was discussed in chapter eight. Truth in the biblical sense is something which must be uncovered. The "truths" which man discovers on his own may have a measure of validity in this world but they are not the eternal realities of God. The truth of God (which is the Lord Himself, Jn. 14:6) can only be uncovered for man by revelation or "unveiling." This unveiling occurs as an act of God when He addresses His Word to man and opens his ears to hear.

The truths which God reveals to man can be divided into three categories. There are the **commissions,** i.e., the imperatives and commands by which God seeks to bring man out of his own way into the way of God. There are the **promises,** i.e., the pledges which indicate the ultimate realities into which the new man in Christ is being drawn by God's grace. And there are the **affirmations,** i.e., the words which are spoken to the heart of believers to strengthen and encourage them in their new being, in the "who-I-am-in-Christ." In all three, in the commands, in the promises and in the affirmations, something is unveiled for man and he sees a particular aspect of the eternal truth of God. The response which is right for any given "truth" would depend upon what was revealed in the unveiling.

Before we discuss the various responses which are appropriate to each of these categories of unveiling it will be helpful to look again at the principle of human behavior from another vantage point. This discussion is being inserted to guard against any legalistic interpretation of the "obedience to the truth" which Peter is suggesting. We discovered three kinds of behavior. The things we do lest others see what we really are we called "cover-up" behavior. The things we do to expose ourselves we called "exposure" behavior. But when we are behaving according to our new nature, when we are simply being who we are in Christ, we called that "expression" behavior. When it is "no longer I who live but Christ who lives in me" (Gal. 2:20) **then the life of the Son is finding expression in the earth.**

This third kind of behavior can only take place as a miracle from above, but it does require a response on the part of man. This response of man is called faith. Biblical faith, however, is more than merely believing in a set of doctrinal propositions. **Faith is a submissive response to the presence of God.** To respond to a doctrinal statement with intellectual agreement might be called faith in some sense of the word but it is not what the Bible calls faith. "For as the body apart from the spirit is dead, so faith apart from works is dead" (Jas. 2:26). By the same token, faithfulness (i.e., the behavior which issues from faith) is more than an obedient response to a code of ethics. **Faithfulness is life lived in the presence of God with meekness and humility.**

Abraham's faith, for example, was not reckoned to him as righteousness simply because he believed that God would give him a son. Many people of our day may believe that God will give them children, but may never have the fulfillment of their desire. That kind of believing does not constitute biblical faith. Abraham's was true faith because it was a submissive response to God who was **present to him in the giving of the promise** (Gen. 15:1-6). Without this presence and this promise Abraham's faith could be no more than a human desire for a son.

Again, Abraham's faithfulness was no mere response to a legal demand. When James asked, "Was not Abraham our father justified by works, when he offered his son Isaac upon the altar?" (Jas. 2:21), he was drawing attention to a situation in which Abraham had responded to instructions received from God in the presence of God (Gen. 22). This event was not an isolated act in which Abraham obeyed a law code. This was the crowning climax of a life lived in submissive obedience to the presence of the speaking God. His whole life was under the determination of the Lord who gave him daily guidance.

Let us illustrate this from the life of Jesus who is the ultimate example of faith and faithfulness. After He healed a man at the pool of Bethesda, the pharisees challenged Him because He did that on the sabbath day. Jesus answered them, "Truly, truly, I say to you, the Son can do nothing of his own accord, but only what he sees the Father doing; for whatever he does, that the Son does likewise" (Jn. 5:19). This indicates that Jesus lived His life as a man **in the presence of God submissively responding to what He saw the Father doing.** When He went into that pool area He had seen a "multitude of invalids" there. If He had been responding to a law code He would have done nothing because it was the Sabbath. The fact that He healed the paralytic indicates that He was responding to the guidance of His Father who wanted to heal. But why did He not heal them all? The clear implication of the text is that He only saw His Father healing one! He did **only** what He saw His Father doing.

Jesus made another statement to His disciples later which is significant in this respect. "I am the vine, you are the branches. He who abides in me, and I in him, he it is that bears much fruit, for **apart from me you can do nothing**" (Jn. 15:5, emphasis mine). As the Son can do nothing apart from the Father, so the "many sons" can do nothing apart from the first-born Son. True faith can be described as seeing (by revelation, or with unveiled face) what He is doing and then acting in a manner which is appropriate to what is seen. This is the way Jesus exercised His faith and this is the way we must exercise our faith. Any attempt to do something or to be something for God which does not issue from this "seeing" is nothing more than a human attempt to please God apart from faith. Obedience of faith is never a response to a legalistic system. It must be a response to God.

Now, getting back to Peter's statement, we notice that the desired response to the truth (i.e., the unveiling) is **obedience.** We have seen that a legalistic interpretation of this word "obedience" would be contrary to the thrust of Jesus and His message. It is possible to render obedience to regulations while inwardly resisting authority. There is no humility or meekness in that kind of obedience. The purifying of the soul can never be accomplished in that way. The outside of the cup may be cleansed, and men may be impressed, but the corruption remains within. That is the kind of shallow hypocrisy against which Jesus pronounced the woes (Matt. 23).

The word translated "obedience" in Peter's exhortation above is literally "under-hearing" (*hupakoe*). This word suggests a more comprehensive concept of obedience than simply doing what is required by laws and commandments. The idea of "hearing" implies that the one who is responding has been **audience to the speaking God.** The Hebrew writer's warning is appropriate here, "See that you do not refuse him who is speaking" (Heb. 12:25). The prefix "under" shows that man's response will be effective for purifying the soul only when he takes his position in meekness under that which is revealed through the unveiling of the truth.

One final question is in order before we return to the issue of the proper response to the various categories of revealed truth. What is it that is purged from the soul in the process of purifying by the obedience to the truth? Our answer is that the soul is purged of those attitudes we have which cause us to take the wrong posture when things do not happen the way we want them to. These attitudes and postures hinder us from responding with faith, hope and love in difficult and threatening situations and relationships. We refer to such things as self-will, passion and the tendency to feel rejected and to reject others.

The first of our categories of truth is the unveiling of God's **commission.** When the truth of God takes the form of a command or a commission, the desired response is the **obedience of faith.** The position of meekness "under" the will of God is first "seeing him who is invisible" (Heb. 11:27) and then doing what the Father is doing. This kind of obedience is possible only in a situation where God is making Himself and His way known to man by removing the veil and allowing man to see what He is doing. This kind of obedience is possible only in a situation where God is making Himself and His way known to man by removing the veil and allowing man to see what He is doing. It can never become a mere system of ethics promoted by the human will apart from the presence of God.

Paul spoke of the **"mystery** which was kept **secret** for long ages but is now **disclosed...**to bring about the **obedience of faith"** (Rom. 16:25,26, emphasis mine). The biblical concept of mystery refers to the realities of God's being and doing which cannot be searched out and known by man. The mystery can only be known when God Himself discloses it to man by opening his eyes to see and his ears to hear. This text from Paul indicates that the purpose of the disclosure (or unveiling) is to bring about the obedience of faith. When the mystery is disclosed in the form of something said, the proper response of man is to "hear-under" what is said. If it is disclosed in the form of something shown the proper response is submission to whatever is seen. In either case the response could be called "obedience of faith" because the response is to the presence of God in the unveiling.

By this submissive hearing of the divine commission received from God Himself the **soul** is **purged** of **self-will** because the behavior is brought under the will of God. After Isaiah had been touched on his lips by the burning coal he was able to say, "Here am I! Lord send me" (Isa. 6:8). He had received an obedient heart and took his rightful position under what he had seen and heard. When he went to preach to those to whom he had been sent he did not alter his posture. He remained in his humble position and spoke only that which was given him by the Lord. Jesus, again our primary example, later expressed it in this way, "...I do nothing on my own authority but speak thus as the Father taught me" (Jn. 8:28). Self-will cannot remain when one is obedient to the truth.

The second of our categories of truth is the unveiling of God's **promises.** When the truth which is unveiled for the new man in Christ takes the form of a promise the desired response will still be to take the position of meekness under that revelation. In this case the "under-hearing" would not be called obedience of faith. The posture one assumes under the revealed promises of God would be called the **obedience of Hope.** The **defilement** of the soul which is **purged** while one is submitted under the truth of God's promises is called **passion.** The connection between hope and passion is not immediately recognizable. Some explanation is needed.

A definition of biblical hope as a response to the revealed promises of God contains two parts. To begin with there is the firm conviction that He who promised is faithful (Heb. 11:11). This is not an optimistic looking on the bright side in a dreamy anticipation of some future utopia. Biblical hope attaches itself behind the veil "as a sure and steadfast anchor of the soul" (Heb. 6:19) to God Himself with the expectation that He will do what He said He would do. **Hope knows that God has already supplied whatever is needed to fulfill His promises.**

The second part of the definition is that there will be a **willingness to wait upon God** and allow Him to choose the **time of fulfillment.** When hope is standing submissively under the unveiled promise of God there will be no anxious exercise of human strength in an attempt to grasp the promise before the time set by the Father.

Passion is a self-seeking drive to find fulfillment for some appetite or desire. In its extreme expression it insists upon having its own way regardless of the cost or burden to others. It considers the desired object to be its rightful possession and will stop at nothing to obtain it. Passion is not satisfied with what might be available at some point in the future. It wants fulfillment now. It will never wait upon God. It does not even expect to receive from Him. "What causes wars, and what causes fightings among you? Is it not your passions that are at war in your members? You desire and do not have; so you kill. And you covet and cannot obtain; so you fight and wage war" (Jas. 4:1,2). What better description could we find for the working of passion.

With these definitions of hope and passion, it is clear that they are in direct conflict with one another. Passion is purged from the soul to the degree that we have received the promises of God in the full assurance of His faithfulness. We have experienced biblical hope when we can say with David, "Thou art my Lord; I have no good apart from thee" (Ps. 16:2), or with Asaph, "Whom have I in heaven but thee? And there is nothing upon earth that I desire besides thee. My flesh and my heart may fail, but God is the strength of my heart and my portion for ever" (Ps. 73:25,26). When God Himself is our portion we can rest in what we have and wait confidently upon Him knowing that He has provided for all our needs "according to his riches in glory in Christ Jesus" (Phil. 4:19). Even if we do not receive what we think we may need in any given situation, it does not really matter because we know that we will someday be "filled with all the fullness of God" (Eph. 3:19).

Our third category of truth is the unveiling of God's **affirmations.** When the truth is unveiled to the believer in the form of affirmation the proper response is **the obedience of love.** The **pollution** of the soul which is **purged** by God's word of affirmation is **Rejection.** Feelings of guilt and condemnation cause us to feel unworthy of acceptance. These feelings are also responsible for our inability to accept others. But when we hear the Lord say, "My son, your sins are forgiven" (Mk. 2:5), something is released deep within the soul. When we understand that we do not have to work ourselves up to a certain level of righteousness before He will accept us, we are set free to receive His unmerited love. But, at the same time, we are set free to love others without demanding that they measure up to our expectations. We are liberated to fulfill His commandment "...love one another as I have loved you" (Jn. 15:12).

This relationship between God's love for us and our love for one another is the thrust of I John 4:7-21 which we quote in part here:

Beloved, let us love one another; for love is of God, and he who loves is born of God and knows God. He who does not love does not know God; for God is love. In this the love of God was made manifest among us, that God sent his only Son into the world, so that we might live through him...Beloved, if God so loved us, we also ought to love one another...So we know and believe the love God has for us. God is love, and he who abides in love abides in God, and God abides in him...We love, because he first loved us.

So, the love of which we speak is not the love of man for God but the love of God for man, the love that prompted Him to give His Son as the sin offering by which man is reconciled to God. When we are secure in His love for us, when we know by the unveiling of the truth of His love, then we can rest in His love and we can love one another with the love with which we have been loved. When we know by revelation that nothing in all creation will be able to separate us from the love of God in Christ Jesus our Lord (Rom. 8:39), when we have our eyes fixed upon the love of God, knowing that He is present in His love, then we will be free to "love one another earnestly from the heart" (I Pet. 1:22). We will have this freedom because our soul will have been purified of rejection by "hearing under" the truth.

We have seen that truth revealed as commission purges the soul of self-will and creates the obedience of faith, that truth revealed as promise purges the soul of passion and produces the obedience of hope, and that truth revealed as affirmation purges the soul of rejection and liberates the new man in Christ to the obedience of love. These three may not be the only forms in which the truth of God may be unveiled, but they are those which establish enduring qualities in the believer. "So faith, hope, love abide, these three; but the greatest of these is love" (I Cor. 13:13).

All this is a result of the fact that God has made Himself present to man through the unveiling of the living and active Word and that man has humbled himself to receive that Word with meekness. This Word received in this way brings salvation to the soul, establishing it under the Spirit of God in health and wholeness so that the new man is free to respond in faith, hope and love to the revealed truth of God.

"Who am I really?" The answer to this question is no longer derived from my earthly parentage or from my involvements in this world as such. I have been born anew.

"Who am I becoming?" I am no longer obligated to look at my failures (or even at my successess) for an answer. I am "being changed into His likeness from one degree of glory to another" and "this comes from the Lord who is the Spirit" (II Cor. 3:18). I do not yet know everything which that might imply, but I am excited about what the future holds in Christ Jesus my Lord. All who have been born of God know that "it does not yet appear what we shall be, but we know that when he appears we shall be like him, for we shall see him as he is. And every one who thus hopes in him purifies himself as he is pure'' (I Jn. 3:2,3).

Not that I have already obtained this or am already perfect; but I press on to make it my own, because Christ has made me His own. Brethren, I do not consider that I have made it my own; but one thing I do, forgetting what lies behind and straining forward to what lies ahead, I press on toward the goal for the prize of the upward call of God in Christ Jesus. **Phil. 3:12-14**